Econometric Model Performance in Forecasting and Policy Assessment

Econometric Model Performance in Forecasting and Policy Assessment

American Enterprise Institute for Public Policy Research
Washington, D.C.

W. Allen Spivey and William J. Wrobleski are professors of statistics at the University of Michigan Graduate School of Business Administration.

Library of Congress Cataloging in Publication Data

Spivey, W Allen.
  Econometric model performance in forecasting and policy assessment.

  (AEI studies; 225)
  Bibliography: p.
  1. Econometrics.   2.   Economic forecasting—Mathematical models.   3.   Economic policy—Mathematical models.
I.   Wrobleski, William J., joint author.   II.   Title.
III.   Series: American Enterprise Institute for Public
Policy Research.   AEI studies; 225.
HB141.S66   330'.01'82   78-21074
ISBN 0-8447-3327-X

AEI Studies 225

Printed in the United States of America

CONTENTS

INTRODUCTION AND OVERVIEW   **1**

1   BASIC CONCEPTS OF LINEAR ECONOMETRIC MODELS   **5**

Structural Form   5

The Reduced Equation Form and Its Role in Forecasting   11

Policy Assessments Using Multipliers and Final Forms   14

The Separated Form   18

2   NONLINEAR ECONOMETRIC MODELS   **21**

Nonlinearities in Econometric Models   21

Forecasts from Nonlinear Models   22

The Gauss-Seidel Algorithm   23

Near-Triangular Rearrangements in Solving Nonlinear Systems   25

3   STUDIES OF FORECAST ERRORS OF MAJOR ECONOMETRIC MODELS   **29**

Previous Major Studies   29

The NBER/NSF Model Comparison Study   31

4 A STUDY OF EX ANTE FORECAST ERRORS
OF THE WHARTON, DRI, CHASE, AND
BEA QUARTERLY ECONOMETRIC MODELS **39**

The Data Base 39
Descriptive Statistics of Ex Ante Forecast Errors 40

5 MAJOR ISSUES OF STATISTICAL INFERENCE
IN ANALYZING FORECASTING PERFORMANCE **47**

Limitations of Descriptive Measures 47
Correlation Structure of Forecast Errors and
Statistical Inference 48

6 POLICY MULTIPLIER STUDIES OF MAJOR
ECONOMETRIC MODELS **51**

Policy Assessments Using Generalized Multipliers 51
The NBER/NSF Model Comparison Study of
Dynamic Policy Multipliers 53
Structural Change in Assessing Policy Multipliers
of Econometric Models 56

APPENDIX **59**

REFERENCES **73**

INTRODUCTION AND OVERVIEW

Large-scale econometric models have received a great deal of attention in academic publications and in the press during the last ten years, and their forecasts and supporting software services appear to be widely used by clients in both industry and government. As a result, there has been an increasing interest in questions related to these models' forecasting performance and their usefulness in assessing alternative economic policies over an intermediate or long-term period.

According to some proponents, large-scale econometric models perform better than alternative means of forecasting, and their policy assessments offer useful guides to decision makers. Critics, on the other hand, have suggested that econometric models do not, by and large, outperform simpler time-series models or forecasts based only on the judgment of individuals or panels. Another group believes that the forecasting record of econometric models is mixed, that the "jury is still out" assessing their forecasting performance, and that the usefulness of these models for policy assessment is at best tenuous.

How does one evaluate econometric model forecasting and policy assessment? The conventional method involves one or more of the following: the analysis of various descriptive measures of forecast errors; the study of turning-point predictions; the investigation of policy assessments, using estimated multipliers; and an examination of other dynamic characteristics of a model through simulation.

This study touches upon these aspects of the evaluation of econometric model performance. It is intended as a guide to the current status of the evaluation of large-scale econometric model forecasting, and it is addressed to persons who use forecasts and policy studies in their work.

1

Such persons have widely different backgrounds, which often do not include formal education in either econometrics or economics. Furthermore, some of the important aspects of model evaluation relate to the methodology employed in developing structural econometric equation systems. Consequently, we present a brief overview of the methodology of linear and nonlinear econometric models and their solution processes in Chapters 1 and 2. This includes a discussion of the judgments the construction of such models inevitably requires, as well as a review of the judgmental considerations involved in generating model forecasts and calculating policy multipliers.

In Chapter 3 we present a summary of the more important findings on econometric model forecasting performance that have been published by both model builders themselves and independent researchers. Then in Chapter 4 we offer our own study of various descriptive measures of quarterly forecast errors from the econometric models of Wharton, Data Resources, Inc. (DRI), Chase Econometric Associates, and the Bureau of Economic Analysis (BEA) of the U.S. Department of Commerce. We discuss the inherent limitations of all published studies of forecast errors of econometric models in Chapter 5, which in many ways is the most important part of this study. Finally, in Chapter 6, we present a brief critique of some studies of the policy multiplier performance of econometric models.

Although Chapters 1 and 2 provide a summary of salient methodological issues in econometric modeling, we have written the remaining chapters in such a way as to require only a limited knowledge of the concepts these chapters present. Thus readers whose principal interests are in empirical studies of econometric model performance and evaluation can proceed directly to Chapters 3 through 6 and should have little difficulty in following the discussion to be found there.

Our conclusions appear at various points in the monograph as they relate to, and are developed from, the discussions which precede them, but a brief statement of our four principal findings will be useful here.

1. All available studies assess the forecasting performance of the major econometric models in terms of root mean square errors (RMSEs) or similar measures. An analysis of these studies shows that rankings based on RMSEs alone change whenever different time periods or different macroeconomic variables are examined. Thus all studies of model performance present merely descriptive measures which relate only to the variables considered and the time periods chosen. These studies do not provide reliable

guides for future model forecasting performance with respect to *levels, changes,* or *turning points,* and no conclusive rankings of model performance can be determined from them.

2. The extensive correlation structure among forecast errors makes it exceedingly difficult to develop statistical inferences, in contrast to descriptive measures limited to a given time period or to a given variable. Statistical inferences are necessary before one can make general statements that permit models to be ranked with reasonable confidence as to expected future forecasting performance. All studies of forecast error performance of the major econometric models have ignored this important issue.

3. Statistical inference in econometric model evaluation is further complicated because only small data bases of comparable observations on forecast errors are available for study. Strictly speaking, these require exact small sample inference procedures for correlated time series before one can rank with confidence the expected future performances of models. At present such statistical theory is not available.

4. No study of econometric models has satisfactorily assessed the long-run performance of policy multipliers. Because such multipliers are merely special kinds of long-run forecasts, their assessment involves all the problems of interpreting forecast performance. Moreover, existing studies are at best descriptive investigations that relate only to specific time periods and to the policy changes selected for examination. They do not establish that multiplier paths calculated from econometric models will bear any reasonable relationship over the long term to the actual effects in the economy that would result from the policy change being investigated.

Our conclusions support the hypothesis that the jury is still out assessing the forecasting performance of econometric models and their use in policy assessment. They support the stronger hypothesis that econometric model evaluation will remain inconclusive until model proprietors make available to the research community forecast error data sets for longer periods of time, and until appropriate methods of statistical inference are applied to them.

These conclusions do not necessarily leave us pessimistic about future prospects of econometric model forecasting, nor are we anti-model. In fact, models can also be evaluated in terms of the cost-benefit trade-offs a model user makes. A model may not forecast well, for example, but it may help a user facing a planning decision gain helpful insights into the possible effects of alternate policies in the short run. Determinations of such benefits can include the conventional approaches of forecast error analyses as well as studies of a model's turning-point performance and its policy assessment features. But they obviously depend in a crucial way on the utility function of the user.

The art and science of large-scale econometric model building had its beginning only in the mid-1950s and is still in its infancy. Research has made important contributions, but much additional work, as indicated at various points in this monograph, remains to be done before econometric model performance can be conclusively evaluated.

1
Basic Concepts of Linear Econometric Models

Structural Form

A structural or behavioral form of an econometric model is a system of equations that expresses the behavior of economic agents or units. Economic theory frequently suggests the nature of such behavior. Variables in a structural form are usually classified into two groups, *endogenous* (dependent) variables, and *exogenous* (independent or explanatory) variables. The former influence other endogenous variables in a system and are in turn influenced by the system. Exogenous variables are regarded as determined by influences outside the system; they affect the endogenous variables, but are not affected directly by them. Examples of exogenous variables are tax rates and similar policy variables. Because economic influences often have impacts on economic agents that extend over several or many time periods, endogenous and exogenous variables can enter a structural form either as concurrent or lagged variables or both.

A typical structural relationship or equation might explain purchases of consumer durable goods in terms of their lagged values as well as in terms of current and lagged values of exogenous variables and still other endogenous variables. A simple example taken from Howrey [29], p. 629, is:

$$
\begin{aligned}
(1) \quad y_1(t) &+ a_{11}y_1(t-1) + a_{20}y_2(t) + a_{21}y_2(t-1) + a_{22}y_2(t-2) \\
&+ a_{23}y_2(t-3) + a_{30}y_3(t) + a_{40}y_4(t) + a_{50}y_5(t) \\
&+ b_{10}x_1(t) + b_{11}x_1(t-1) + b_{12}x_1(t-2) = u_1(t)
\end{aligned}
$$

where the y's indicate the dependent or endogenous variables of the system, the x's indicate the independent or exogenous variables and where

$$y_1(t) = \text{purchases of consumer durables in the current period } t$$

$y_1(t-1) = $ purchases of consumer durables in the previous period $t-1$ (this is a lagged value of y_1, sometimes referred to as y_1 lagged one period)

$y_2(t) = $ personal disposable income in the current period

$y_2(t-j) = $ personal disposable income in period $t-j$ for $j = 1, 2, 3$

$y_3(t) = $ unemployment rate in current period

$y_4(t) = $ implicit price deflator for consumer durable goods in current period

$y_5(t) = $ implicit price deflator for consumption for the current period

$x_1(t) = $ stock of consumer durable goods in current period

$x_1(t-j) = $ stock of consumer durable goods in period $t-j$ for $j = 1, 2$

$u_1(t) = $ a random shock or error associated with the structural equation.

The subscript i of the coefficients a_{ij} associated with the lagged endogenous variables $y_i(t-j)$ designates the variable with which it is associated, and the index j designates the lag (where we include $j = 0$ to denote the current value). This subscripting convention is also used with the coefficients b_{ij} of the exogenous variables.

Equation (1) can be thought of as an attempt to explain consumer durable goods purchases $y_1(t)$ in the current period in terms of some endogenous variables and an exogenous variable. In this example the endogenous variables include consumer durable goods purchases lagged one and two periods, current and lagged values of personal disposable income, the unemployment rate, as well as two price influences (the implicit price deflators for consumer durable goods and for consumption), the last three variables referring to the current period only. The exogenous variable is the stock of consumer durable goods in the current period, together with its given lagged values. The random shock $u_1(t)$ in (1) indicates that the relationship between the variables is not assumed to be known exactly, but is subject to errors that are modeled by random variables having a specified probability structure.

In an econometric model containing (1) there would be other structural equations which explain each of the current endogenous variables in (1) in terms of still other endogenous and exogenous variables in the system. As new current endogenous variables arise in these equations, they must be explained in turn through still other structural equations or, at some point in the model-building process, they must be classified as predetermined variables and grouped with the exogenous variables of the system. The system is called *complete* when the number of structural equations is equal to the number of current endogenous variables not classified as predetermined, and when the system can be solved for these endogenous variables.

The equation system (1) can be rewritten by using the lag operator L, where for any variable v, $Lv(t) = v(t-1)$ or more generally $L^k v(t) = v(t-k)$, $k = 0, 1, 2, \cdots$. Equation (1) then becomes

(2) $\quad y_1(t) + a_{11} L y_1(t) + a_{20} y_2(t) + a_{21} L y_2(t) + a_{22} L^2 y_2(t)$
$\qquad + a_{23} L^3 y_2(t) + a_{30} y_3(t) + a_{40} y_4(t) + a_{50} y_5(t)$
$\qquad + b_{10} x_1(t) + b_{11} L x_1(t) + b_{12} L^2 x_1(t) = u_1(t).$

Factoring the common y's and x's gives rise to coefficients for these variables which are polynomial expressions in the lag operator L, and (2) becomes

$$(1 + a_{11} L) y_1(t) + (a_{20} + a_{21} L + a_{22} L^2 + a_{23} L^3) y_2(t)$$
$$+ a_{30} y_3(t) + a_{40} y_4(t) + a_{50} y_5(t) + (b_{10} + b_{11} L$$
$$+ b_{12} L^2) x_1(t) = u_1(t).$$

This can be written compactly as

(3) $\quad a_1(L) y_1(t) + a_2(L) y_2(t) + a_3(L) y_3(t) + a_4(L) y_4(t)$
$\qquad + a_5(L) y_5(t) + b_1(L) x_1(t) = u_1(t)$

where $a_1(L) = 1 + a_{11} L$
$\qquad a_2(L) = a_{20} + a_{21} L + a_{22} L^2 + a_{23} L^3$
$\qquad a_3(L) = a_{30}$
$\qquad a_4(L) = a_{40}$
$\qquad a_5(L) = a_{50}$
$\qquad b_1(L) = b_{10} + b_{11} L + b_{12} L^2.$

As indicated earlier, each endogenous variable would be related to other variables through its own structural equation, which would be written in form (1) or in form (3), using appropriate lag operators. To consider the general case, suppose the equation system contains g current endogenous variables that are being explained in a model having k exogenous variables (it being understood that any predetermined variables are classified as exogenous variables), and assume that the maximum lags associated with the endogenous and exogenous variables are r periods and s periods respectively. Then a linear econometric equation system can be written as

(4) $A_0 y(t) + A_1 y(t-1) + \cdots + A_r y(t-r) + B_0 x(t) + B_1 x(t-1)$
$\qquad + \cdots + B_s x(t-s) = u(t)$

where $y(t)$ is a g by 1 vector of current endogenous variables, $x(t)$ is a k by 1 vector of exogenous variables, and $u(t)$ is a g by 1 vector of random shocks or equation disturbances having mean zero and constant variance-covariance matrix Σ. In addition, the disturbances $u(t)$ are assumed to be uncorrelated with $x(t)$ as well as with the vector of disturbances for other time periods. The latter property means that the $u(t)$ are uncorrelated over time or are serially uncorrelated. However, the components of the vector $u(t)$ are correlated for a given t, and it is this contemporaneous correlation structure among the random equation disturbances that is specified by the variance-covariance matrix Σ. It is understood that identities may be appended to (4).

By using the lag operator L the equation (4) can be written as

$$(A_0 + A_1 L + \cdots + A_r L^r)y(t) + (B_0 + B_1 L + \cdots + B_s L^s)x(t) = u(t)$$

or more compactly as

(5)
$$A(L)y(t) + B(L)x(t) = u(t)$$

where

(6)
$$A(L) = A_0 + A_1 L + \cdots + A_r L^r$$

and

(7)
$$B(L) = B_0 + B_1 L + \cdots + B_s L^s.$$

Thus $A(L)$ is a g by g matrix, $B(L)$ is a g by k matrix and each of these matrices has as its elements polynomials in the operator L. The equation system (4), or its operator representation (5) together with (6) and (7), is called the *structural form of a linear econometric model*.

When the structural form (4) or the operator representation (5), together with (6) and (7), is used to model macroeconomic activity, its generality is restricted by placing conditions on its coefficient matrices. For example, the matrix A_0 in (4), which corresponds to the current endogenous variables explained by the model (those with zero lag), will be a nondiagonal matrix reflecting the simultaneity of the system. In equation (1), for example, personal disposable income and the unemployment rate influence the purchase of consumer durables in the current period, and the unemployment rate also influences current personal disposable income. At the same time, the model does not allow purchases of consumer durables to influence either personal disposable income or unemployment in the current period. Thus, although A_0 is nondiagonal, it will often contain many zero elements, each of which indicates that some current endogenous variable is not present in the structural relationship to explain some other current endogenous variable. Another restriction on A_0 is that one can determine the coefficients in the structural form only up to a factor of

8

proportionality unless some normalization rule is employed. For convenience, the matrix A_0 in (4) is usually subjected to a normalization whereby its diagonal elements are assumed to be equal to one; such a normalization is present in (1) and (4), where the coefficient of $y_1(t)$ is set equal to one.

One relies on economic theory to assist in specifying the nature of the structural form as well as in choosing the variables to be included or excluded from a given behavioral equation belonging to an econometric model. This process of including and excluding variables from an equation is also related to the *identifiability of the equation* in a structural form. An aspect of identifiability is the placing of restrictions on some of the elements of the coefficient matrices in (4). These restrictions usually take the form of setting specific elements of these matrices equal to zero and are often referred to as zero restrictions. This is equivalent to the exclusion being guided by a priori knowledge of economic relationships.

A suitably broad context for examining the concept of identifiability requires the recognition that (4) is a *stochastic* linear equation system. Thus we must be concerned not only with the imposition of appropriate zero restrictions but also with the joint probability density function of the endogenous variables $y(t)$ conditional upon the exogenous variables of the system. The parameters of this joint density are related to the parameters of the system (4), the latter being the elements of the matrices A_j, B_i, and Σ, the variance-covariance matrix of the system. When there is a one-to-one correspondence between the parameters of the structural form and the parameters of the conditional joint density of the current endogenous variables (more precisely, when there is a bijective mapping between the former parameter space and the latter) the *structural form* is said to be *identifiable*. We will return to a brief consideration of these issues in the next section.

The matrices A_1, A_2, $\cdots$, A_r and B_1, B_2, $\cdots$, B_s in (4) represent lagged influences of both endogenous and exogenous variables on the current endogenous variables. Unfortunately, economic theory provides little insight into the dynamic nature of these lagged relationships. That is, theory does not clearly specify the number of lags r and s to choose in a structural form, nor, for a given choice of r and s, is the problem of inclusion and exclusion of lagged variables unambiguously resolved. Furthermore, theory does not often specify either the magnitudes or the signs of such lagged effects. For example, in the equation (1) macroeconomic theory does not indicate how many lagged terms of personal disposable income to include. Perhaps the exogenous variable, stock of consumer durable goods, should be lagged for only one period rather than two, or perhaps other exogenous variables should be included.

In addition, the presence of lagged variables in (4) may lead to the problem of *multicollinearity*. The problem exists whenever there are linear relationships among explanatory variables. Such relationships dilute the explanatory power of these variables, they may produce misleading inferences concerning model parameters, and they also may cause considerable computational difficulty in estimation. For these reasons the problem is a serious one in applied econometrics.

The great variety of difficult modeling problems arising in the specification of the coefficient matrices in (4) account for many of the differences between the lag structures of the equations found in the major econometric models of the American economy. There are also major differences in the classification of variables into endogenous and exogenous or predetermined variables. Even when the endogenous variables are common to two or more models, the patterns of inclusion and exclusion of the current endogenous variables from equation to equation can be materially different.

These differences, which are part of the specification problem of econometrics, make it extremely difficult to compare and rank econometric models on the basis of either forecast error performance or policy assessment. Moreover, because of these differences some models may perform better than others at some stages of the business cycle;

TABLE 1

SOME DATA ON MODEL SIZES

(number)

Model	Stochastic Equations	Identities	Endogenous Variables	Exogenous Variables
BEA (1970)[a]	58	41	99	83
Data Resources, Inc. (1970)	200	168	368	120
Federal Reserve Bank of St. Louis	5	4	9	3
Wharton Mark III (circa 1970)	67	134	201	104

[a] BEA denotes the econometric model of the Bureau of Economic Analysis of the U.S. Department of Commerce.

SOURCE: Fromm and Klein [21], pp. 388–391.

10

TABLE 2

Total Number of Equations for Selected Econometric Models

Model	1970	1974
BEA	99	117
Data Resources, Inc.	368	698
Federal Reserve Bank of St. Louis	9	9
Wharton Mark III	201	191
Chase Econometric Associates	NA	403

NA: Not available.
SOURCE: Christ [9], p. 58; data on Chase model from private communication.

they may respond differently to inflation and monetary effects, to major random shocks such as an energy crisis, or to a major financial dislocation such as a severe credit squeeze. A further difficulty lies in the fact that econometricians continuously alter their models, varying the specification of endogenous and exogenous variables, the lag structures of each, the degree of disaggregation, and so forth.

Table 1 offers an impression of the differences in size and in the number of endogenous and exogenous variables for some of the well-known econometric models. Table 2 gives some information about changes in the total number of equations for selected econometric models over several years. These changes often make it very difficult to compare the forecast error performance and policy assessment features of even the same model over two different periods of time.

The Reduced Equation Form and Its Role in Forecasting

The structural form (4), or its operator representation (5) together with (6) and (7), provides an *implicit* functional form. It is often convenient, particularly for forecasting purposes, to restate (4) so that the current endogenous variables $y(t)$ appear as explicit functions of the lagged endogenous variables, the exogenous and predetermined variables, and the random disturbances $u(t)$. For systems that are linear in the coefficients, the implicit function theorem reduces to the requirement that the matrix A_0 in (4), which corresponds to the zero lags, has an inverse A_0^{-1}. The existence of such an inverse is assured

11

when a structural form is complete. Given the completeness of (4) we can obtain a *reduced form* as

$$y(t) = -A_0^{-1}[A_1 y(t-1) + \cdots + A_r y(t-r) + B_0 x(t) \\ + B_1 x(t-1) + \cdots + B_s x(t-s)] + A_0^{-1} u(t)$$

or simply

$$(8) \qquad y(t) = C_1 y(t-1) + \cdots + C_r y(t-r) + D_0 x(t) + \cdots \\ + D_s x(t-s) + \epsilon(t),$$

where $\epsilon(t) = A_0^{-1} u(t)$ and

$$(9) \qquad\qquad C_j = -A_0^{-1} A_j \qquad j = 1, \cdots, r$$

$$(10) \qquad\qquad D_i = -A_0^{-1} B_i \qquad i = 0, \cdots, s.$$

In addition to the completeness condition for the structural form, which assures its solution in terms of $y(t)$, the identifiability of an equation of the structural form can be examined in terms of the relationship between its coefficients and those in the reduced form.

Standard econometric textbooks present necessary and sufficient conditions under which the coefficients of the linear structural form can be determined uniquely from those of the reduced form (see Theil [46], pp. 489–495, Johnston [32], pp. 352–361, and Klein [35], pp. 137–145). Econometricians also distinguish between exact identification, overidentification, and underidentification (see, for example, Theil [46], pp. 448–451).

The reduced form plays a central role in producing a forecast. To define a forecast developed from an econometric model, we need the concept of conditional mean of the endogenous variables $y(t)$ or, more accurately, the expected value of $y(t)$, given its previous lagged values and the current and lagged exogenous variables. We first observe that the random equation disturbances in (8), $\epsilon(t) = A_0^{-1} u(t)$, are linear combinations of the random shocks of the structural form (4). Also, given the assumptions concerning $u(t)$,

$$E[u(t)|y(t-1), \cdots, y(t-r), x(t), \cdots, x(t-s)] = 0,$$

and therefore the conditional mean of $\epsilon(t)$ is zero as well. Thus the conditional mean of the endogenous variables in (8) is

$$(11) \quad E[y(t)|y(t-1), \cdots, y(t-r), x(t), \cdots, x(t-s)] \\ = C_1 y(t-1) + \cdots + C_r y(t-r) + D_0 x(t) + \cdots + D_s x(t-s).$$

If at time t one wishes to develop a forecast of the values of the endogenous variables for τ steps ahead, one uses the expression for the conditional mean (11) as follows. First, the coefficient matrices

C_j and D_i are replaced by their statistical estimates developed from data of the sample period to which the model is fitted. Second, the model builder must supply specific values for the exogenous variables for each of the periods $t+1, \cdots, t+\tau$. These values can be developed by means of forecasts from so-called hidden models or from other judgmental considerations. Third, given such values $\hat{x}(t+1), \cdots,$ $\hat{x}(t+\tau)$, then (11) is used iteratively to produce estimates of the requisite (lagged) values of the endogenous variables. For example, a model forecast $\hat{y}_f(t+1)$ of $y(t+1)$ for the period $t+1$ is given by

$$(12) \quad \hat{y}_f(t+1) = \hat{C}_1 y(t) + \hat{C}_2 y(t-1) + \cdots + \hat{C}_r y(t-r+1) \\ + \hat{D}_0 \hat{x}(t+1) + \hat{D}_1 x(t) + \cdots + \hat{D}_s x(t-s+1),$$

where $\hat{C}_j$ and $\hat{D}_i$ denote estimated matrices. Then for period $t+2$ the model forecast is

$$(13) \quad \hat{y}_f(t+2) = \hat{C}_1 \hat{y}_f(t+1) + \hat{C}_2 y(t) + \cdots + \hat{C}_r y(t-r+2) \\ + \hat{D}_0 \hat{x}(t+2) + \hat{D}_1 \hat{x}(t+1) + \cdots + \hat{D}_s x(t-s+2).$$

The remaining forecasts are developed similarly, with the future forecasts being influenced not only by the forecasted (or otherwise specified) values of the exogenous variables but also by the forecasted values of the required endogenous variables as well as by the estimated coefficient matrices. Such forecasts of the future values of the endogenous variables are called *ex ante* forecasts. Because the actual values of the exogenous variables are usually unknown at the time forecasts are made, estimated values of these variables are often used, and the resulting forecasts are called *conditional ex ante* forecasts.

In practice, model builders frequently compensate for departures from the random disturbance assumptions of zero mean and absence of serial correlation from period to period by including empirically or judgmentally developed additive and multiplicative adjustment factors in the forecast equations. They also assess the model forecasts of $y(t)$ using subjective judgments and may make further changes in the forecasted values of the exogenous variables in addition to possible further additive and multiplicative error adjustments. New forecasts of the endogenous variables are then generated, and interactions between the model builder and model may continue until the econometrician obtains forecasts that satisfy his or her judgmental criteria. The published forecasts, usually the result of such an interactive, judgmental process, can be as much a product of the model builder's informed intuition as they are of the model's formal structure and properties.

Frequently, for diagnostic and other purposes, the model builder will often divide a past period into a sample period and a forecast test period. The econometric model is then estimated using data from the sample period, and its forecasting properties during the forecast test period are examined by comparing forecasts of the endogenous variables for this period with the actual values of these variables which are, of course, known. Such forecasts of the endogenous variable are called *unconditional ex post* forecasts.

As indicated earlier, developing forecasts from (11) requires estimation of the unknown coefficient matrices C_j and D_i. In practice these are often obtained by first estimating the coefficients of the matrices A_0, A_j, and B_i in the structural form, and then using the relations (9) and (10) to obtain estimates of the C_j and D_i. Many estimation methods are available for this purpose, ranging from such single equation methods as two-stage least squares and limited information maximum likelihood to full systems methods. The latter methods of estimation reflect more comprehensively the structural interrelationships imposed by the econometric model than do the single equation methods.

Ordinary least squares methods, when applied to (4) on an equation-by-equation basis, usually will not lead even to consistent estimators of the equation parameters, because when an equation is regarded as standing alone for purposes of estimation, feedback influences from the remaining equations are ignored. This in turn causes the residuals of the equation to be correlated with its explanatory variables, thus violating an assumption of no correlation made earlier when discussing the structural form (4). Other estimation methods indicated above, however, do not have this defect; they produce consistent estimators that possess other desirable statistical properties as well.

Despite the variety of estimation methods available, model builders often use the simpler single equation methods (usually two-stage least squares) combined with ordinary least squares (Fromm and Klein [21], pp. 388–391). Differences in methods of estimation obviously produce differences in forecasts, and they further complicate the assessment of forecast performance across models.

Policy Assessments Using Multipliers and Final Forms

When a linear econometric model is used in policy assessment, it is interesting to examine the impacts over time of policy changes on the endogenous variables of the model. Policy changes can have an immediate or current impact as well as delayed or interim impacts on endogenous variables; the latter result from the transmission of the effects of policy changes through the lag structures of the model as they express themselves through time. Economists often call the delayed impacts *dynamic effects* and refer to the immediate impacts as *static effects*. One may also be interested in the total or cumulative impact of a policy change sustained over a sequence of periods. The various impacts—immediate, delayed, and cumulative—can be assessed by means of *policy multipliers*.

If there are no lagged endogenous variables among the predetermined variables in a reduced form, then the reduced form itself provides a description of the evolution of the econometric model over time and hence may be used to examine the effects of policy changes (in the form of changes in exogenous variables) over time. If lagged endogenous variables appear among the predetermined variables, however, the effects of a change in an exogenous variable cannot be directly assessed from the reduced form. The principal reason for this is that effects of such a change extend into the future through the dynamic structure of the model, because the current endogenous variables become the next period's lagged endogenous variables and hence will influence the current endogenous variables of the subsequent period. To put it another way, when lagged endogenous variables appear among the endogenous variables, the structural form (5) is a system of linear stochastic difference equations with constant coefficients, and the lagged values of the endogenous variables must be eliminated by reexpressing them in terms of exogenous variables alone. This leads to the *final form* of an econometric model which we now proceed to develop.

Suppressing the constant term in (8), if any, because it does not affect multiplier considerations, and for simplicity restricting (8) to the special case of a one-period lag in the endogenous and exogenous variables, we can rewrite (8) as

$$(14) \qquad y(t) = C_1 y(t-1) + D_0 x(t) + D_1 x(t-1) + \epsilon(t),$$

where $\epsilon(t) = A_0^{-1} u(t)$. Using the expression for $y(t-1)$ provided by (14) and eliminating $y(t-1)$ from (14) by substitution gives

$$(15) \quad \begin{aligned} y(t) &= C_1 [C_1 y(t-2) + D_0 x(t-1) + D_1 x(t-2) + \epsilon(t-1)] \\ &\quad + D_0 x(t) + D_1 x(t-1) + \epsilon(t) \\ &= C_1^2 y(t-2) + D_0 x(t) + (C_1 D_0 + D_1) x(t-1) \\ &\quad + C_1 D_1 x(t-2) + \epsilon(t) + C_1 \epsilon(t-1). \end{aligned}$$

Substituting into (15) the expression provided from (14) for $y(t-2)$ and continuing until all of the lagged endogenous variables are replaced in this fashion gives

$$(16) \quad y(t) = D_0 x(t) + \sum_{j=1}^{\infty} C_1^{j-1} (C_1 D_0 + D_1) x(t-j) + \sum_{j=0}^{\infty} C_1 \epsilon(t-j),$$

where $C_1^0 = I$.

The system (16), which is called the *final form*, should be contrasted with the reduced form (14) or its structural form. Equation (16) expresses the current endogenous variables $y(t)$ in terms of the current and lagged exogenous variables only, whereas in the reduced and structural forms $y(t)$ is expressed in terms of the lagged endogenous as well as the current and lagged exogenous variables. Moreover, the conditional mean of $y(t)$ from (16), given the current and past values of the exogenous variables, is

$$(17) \qquad E[y(t)|x(t), x(t-1), \cdots] = D_0 x(t)$$

$$+ \sum_{j=1}^{\infty} C_1^{j-1}(C_1 D_0 + D_1) x(t-j).$$

Various *policy multipliers* can be calculated from the conditional expectation (17). For example, the matrix M_0 of *impact multipliers* consists of the partial derivatives of the conditional mean of each of the endogenous variables $y_i(t)$ with respect to each of the current exogenous variables $x_j(t)$,

$$(18) \qquad \frac{\partial E[y_i(t)|x(t), x(t-1), \cdots]}{\partial x_j(t)} = d_0^{ij}, \quad \begin{array}{l} i = 1, 2, \cdots, g \\ j = 1, 2, \cdots, k \end{array}$$

where d_0^{ij} is the i, j element of the matrix D_0 in (17), that is,

$$(19) \qquad\qquad\qquad M_0 = D_0.$$

In contrast to the "infinitesimal" change expressed in (18), suppose that each of the elements of the current exogenous vector $x(t)$ is changed or incremented by one unit to obtain $x(t) + \underset{\sim}{1}$, where $\underset{\sim}{1}$ is a k by 1 vector each of whose components is equal to 1. This change is transmitted through the econometric model as specified by its structural form and results in changes in the conditional mean of $y(t)$. These latter changes are related to the instantaneous impact multipliers as follows:

$$E[y(t)|x(t) + \underset{\sim}{1}, x(t-1), \cdots] - E[y(t)|x(t), x(t-1), \cdots]$$
$$= D_0 \underset{\sim}{1} = M_0 \underset{\sim}{1}.$$

Now let M_1 be the matrix of partial derivatives of the conditional mean of the endogenous variables with respect to the exogenous variables lagged one period. M_1 is called the matrix of one-period *interim multipliers* of the econometric model. From (17) we see that

(20) $$M_1 = C_1 D_0 + D_1,$$

and if M_k is the matrix of k period interim multipliers consisting of the partial derivatives of the conditional mean of the endogenous variables with respect to the endogenous variables lagged k periods, then

(21) $$M_k = C_1^{k-1}(C_1 D_0 + D_1) \qquad k = 1, 2, \cdots.$$

Finally, the total or cumulated multiplier matrix is

(22) $$M = \sum_{k=0}^{\infty} M_k$$

$$= D_0 + \sum_{j=1}^{\infty} C_1^{j-1}(C_1 D_0 + D_1)$$

$$= D_0 + (\sum_{j=1}^{\infty} C_1^{j})D_0 + (\sum_{j=1}^{\infty} C_1^{j-1})D_1$$

$$= (I + \sum_{j=1}^{\infty} C_1^{j})D_0 + (\sum_{j=1}^{\infty} C_1^{j-1})D_1$$

$$= (I - C_1)^{-1}(D_0 + D_1).$$

A necessary and sufficient condition that $\sum_{j=0}^{\infty} C_1^{j}$ exists and equals $(I - C_1)^{-1}$ is that all of the characteristic roots of the matrix C_1, that is, all the roots of $|C_1 - \lambda I| = 0$, lie within the unit circle. This condition is satisfied whenever the structural form corresponding to (14) is *stable*, that is, when all the roots of $|A(z)| = 0$ lie outside the unit circle, where in the special case of one-period lags $A(z) = A_0 + A_1 z$.

The preceding development of explicit expressions for the impact, interim, and total multipliers was based on the use of the conditional expectation (17), which was in turn associated with the final form (16). Analogous explicit expressions for the impact and interim multipliers in the general case of a linear structural econometric model in which there are lags of r periods in the endogenous variables and lags of s periods in the exogenous variables can be developed in a straightforward manner (Brissimis [6]) and are given by

$$M_0 = D_0$$

(23)
$$M_i = \sum_{n=0}^{i} C(n)D_{i-n} \qquad 1 \leqq i \leqq s$$

$$M_{s+j} = \sum_{n=0}^{s} C(j+n)D_{s-n}, \; j \geqq 1$$

where for each n we have

$$C(n) = \sum_{m=1}^{r} C_m C(n-m),$$

where C_m is the coefficient matrix of $y(t-m)$ in the reduced form (8) and where $C(0) = I$, $C(-1) = 0$, $C(-2) = 0$, $\cdots$, I and 0 being g by g matrices.

The Separated Form

Solving the operator representation of the structural form (5) for $y(t)$ we obtain the *final form* of a linear econometric model,

(24)
$$y(t) = -[A(L)]^{-1}B(L)x(t) + [A(L)]^{-1}u(t),$$

where $[A(L)]^{-1}$ is the inverse of the operator $A(L)$. The existence of $[A(L)]^{-1}$ is assured when the system is *stable*. The final form (16), developed for a linear model having one-period lags, is an alternative representation of (24). Recalling that

(25)
$$[A(L)]^{-1} = \frac{adj[A(L)]}{|A(L)|},$$

where $adj[A(L)]$ is the adjoint matrix of $A(L)$ and $|A(L)|$ is the determinant of $A(L)$, (24) can be rewritten as

(26)
$$|A(L)|y(t) = -adj[A(L)]B(L)x(t) + adj[A(L)]u(t).$$

The system (26) differs from both the reduced form (8) and the final form (24) by reintroducing lags in the endogenous variables, but in

18

a special way that is useful for some purposes. To see this, note that $|A(L)|$ must be a polynomial in L, say,

$$|A(L)| = a_0 + a_1 L + \cdots + a_p L^p;$$

thus the left-hand side of (26) is a vector whose j^{th} component can be written as

$$|A(L)|y_j(t) = (a_0 + a_1 L + \cdots + a_p L^p)y_j(t)$$
$$= a_0 y_j(t) + a_1 y_j(t-1) + \cdots + a_p y_j(t-p).$$

Therefore the lag structure of the current endogenous variable in (26) has been "separated" or disengaged in such a way that $y_j(t)$ is influenced only by its own lagged values $y_j(t-1)$, $\cdots$, $y_j(t-p)$, and not by current or lagged values of other endogenous variables. For this reason (26) is referred to as the *separated form* of the linear econometric model.[1] The separated form can be contrasted with both the structural form (4) and the reduced form (8). In each equation of the latter an endogenous variable $y_j(t)$ can be influenced by its own lagged values as well as by the current and lagged values of other endogenous variables.

Recent research by Zellner and Palm [55, 56] has suggested that there is a useful interplay between the fields of time series analysis and multiple equation econometrics. In the past these fields have not been looked upon as being closely allied. The point of contact between the two fields is the separated form (26) which can be regarded as an autoregressive-moving average time series model of the transfer function type.

---

[1] Equations (24) and (26) have been referred to in the literature in a variety of ways. Theil and Boot [47] referred to (24) as the final form, and Jorgenson [33] called it a system of rational distributed lag equations; Tinbergen [48] referred to (26) as the final equations, and Marshak [40] called (26) the separated form. Zellner and Palm [55] called (26) the transfer equations and Klein [36] referred to them as the final form. Equations (26) are also called the autoregressive final form by Dhrymes [11] and the fundamental dynamic equations associated with the reduced form by Kmenta [37].

2

Nonlinear Econometric Models

Nonlinearities in Econometric Models

Although linear models are a useful starting point for examining the major concepts of econometric model building, all the large econometric models in use today are nonlinear in variables and contain nonlinear structural relationships as well. Nonlinearities in the endogenous and exogenous variables are present in the form of powers, ratios, logarithms, and so on. Any variable which is expressed in constant dollars in a model, for example, is the ratio of two other variables in the system, one expressed in terms of nominal or current dollars and the other an appropriate implicit price deflator. Income sectors typically contain other types of nonlinearities in variables. These arise, for example, when models are sufficiently detailed so that wage rates, hours of work, and employment are expressed as endogenous variables through individual behavioral equations at the industry level. Wage payments for an industry can then be obtained from the triple product of these three endogenous variables, and these products are summed over the industries represented in the model to form total wage and salary payments. Nonlinear behavioral relations are also found in each of the major models. Logarithmic relationships for wage and price determination are common and are important for the modeling of inflationary responses as employment and capacity ceilings are approached.

A general nonlinear structural equation system relating the current and lagged endogenous variables, the current and lagged exogenous and predetermined variables, the random equation shocks, and the parameters of the econometric system can be written implicitly in the form

(27) $G[y(t), y(t-1), \cdots, y(t-r), x(t), \cdots, x(t-s), u(t); \Omega] = 0$

where Ω is a set of parameters associated with the model. Assumptions could be made which permit the application of the implicit function theorem so that (27) could be solved explicitly and simultaneously for the current endogenous variables $y(t)$ as

(28) $y(t) = F[y(t-1), \cdots, y(t-r), x(t), \cdots, x(t-s), u(t); \Phi]$,

where Φ is a set of parameters corresponding to Ω in (27). A simplifying assumption that the errors $u(t)$ in (28) are additive could then be employed, giving what we call the nonlinear reduced form with additive errors,

(29) $y(t) = H[y(t-1), \cdots, y(t-r), x(t), \cdots, x(t-s); \Phi] + u(t)$.

As with linear econometric models, questions arise as to the identifiability of the systems (27), (28), or (29) and the estimability of their parameters. These issues are even more difficult to resolve in the case of nonlinear models, and a general treatment analogous to that for the linear structural econometric model does not exist, although some estimation results are available (Amemiya [1]; Berndt, Hall, Hall, and Hausman [5]; and Jorgenson and Laffont [34]).

Forecasts from Nonlinear Models

The development of a forecast from a nonlinear model would be analogous to that in the linear case when the nonlinear reduced form (29) corresponding to the linear reduced form (8) can be obtained. Except in special cases, however, analytical methods are not available for nonlinear systems to obtain (28) or (29) in which the simultaneous solutions $y(t)$ to (27) are expressed explicitly in functional form. For this reason, the general nonlinear structural form (27) itself must be employed to generate model forecasts. To develop forecasts for periods $t+1, \cdots, t+\tau$ for nonlinear econometric models, values of the exogenous and predetermined variables for each of these periods are required. We denote these as $\hat{x}(t+1), \cdots, \hat{x}(t+\tau)$. Using these values and setting the random shock terms $u(t+1) = 0, \cdots, u(t+\tau) = 0$, we would obtain the forecasted values $\hat{y}_f(t+1), \cdots, \hat{y}_f(t+\tau)$ of the endogenous variables as numerical solutions of the recursively related, nonlinear equation systems

$$G[\hat{y}_f(t+1), y(t), \cdots, y(t-r+1), \hat{x}(t+1), x(t), \cdots,$$
$$x(t-s+1), 0; \Omega] = 0$$

(30)

$$G[\hat{y}_f(t+\tau), \cdots, \hat{x}(t+\tau), \cdots, 0; \Omega] = 0.$$

The numerical values for $\hat{y}_f(t+1)$, the one-step forecasts, from the first system in (30) depend on the lagged values of the endogenous variables, the values of the exogenous and predetermined variables, the nonlinear relationships G chosen to model the system, and the parameter set Ω, whose elements must be estimated.

The forecasts $\hat{y}_f(t+1)$ for the first period are used in the second system of (30) along with the other variables indicated to determine numerical values of $\hat{y}_f(t+2)$, the two-step-ahead forecasts. Then both $\hat{y}_f(t+1)$ and $\hat{y}_f(t+2)$ are used in the third system of (30) to obtain the three-step-ahead forecasts, and this process is continued until the final system in (30) is solved for the numerical values $\hat{y}_f(t+\tau)$, giving the τ-step-ahead forecasts. Thus the sequence of interlocking numerical solutions $\hat{y}_f(t+1)$, $\cdots$, $\hat{y}_f(t+\tau)$ to the nonlinear equation systems comprising (30) would be the forecasts for the periods $t+1$, $\cdots$, $t+\tau$, and they provide a dynamic solution path of the econometric model over the chosen forecast horizon.

For large models, of course, numerical solutions of (30) require computer-based algorithms, which effectively exploit the specific non-linear structural relationships that are used. Because economic theory provides little insight into functional specifications of such nonlinear relationships, these are often developed in practice from empirical studies. The specifications of the nonlinearities found in existing major models are mainly dealt with in an ad hoc manner and rely on the experience and judgments of the model builder even more than in the linear case. Thus in current econometric practice the nonlinearities typically encountered are not mathematically complicated, and they often turn out to be of special analytical forms which facilitate the development of numerical solutions. For these reasons, matters relating to the development, application, and use of numerical algorithms for solving mathematically complicated nonlinear systems are not of central importance to econometricians currently. Instead, they are able to use simpler numerical methods, principally the Gauss-Seidel algorithm, to develop numerical solutions for their nonlinear econometric models.

The Gauss-Seidel Algorithm

In order to discuss how the Gauss-Seidel algorithm is applied to non-linear econometric models to obtain forecasts, consider (27), in which the random shocks have been set equal to zero,

(31) $\quad G[y(t), y(t-1), \cdots, y(t-r), x(t), \cdots, x(t-s), 0; \Omega] = 0.$

Application of the Gauss-Seidel algorithm to (31) requires that each of the g endogenous variables $y_j(t)$ be expressed as a function of the other variables of the system as

$$y_1(t) = h_1[y_2(t), \cdots, y_g(t), y(t-1), \cdots, y(t-r), x(t), \cdots,$$
$$x(t-s); \Phi_1]$$
$$y_2(t) = h_2[y_1(t), \cdots, y_g(t), y(t-1), \cdots, y(t-r), x(t), \cdots,$$
$$x(t-s); \Phi_2]$$

(32)

$$y_g(t) = h_g[y_1(t), \cdots, y_{g-1}(t), y(t-1), \cdots, y(t-r), x(t), \cdots,$$
$$x(t-s); \Phi_g].$$

The equations (32), of course, are not the simultaneous solutions of (31) but merely express a single endogenous variable as a function of the remaining variables. It should be noted that there may be several equations in (31) which could be solved for a given endogenous variable. Not every choice of equations of the type (32) will lead, in the application of the Gauss-Seidel algorithm, to a sequence of values that converges to a solution of the system (31) when the latter exists. The problem of choosing the equations (32) so as to obtain convergence is often referred to as the normalization of the equation system.

The problem of normalization causes few difficulties in practice, because if a nonconvergent choice for (32) is made by the model builder, the algorithm would generally signal that such a choice has been made, and the model builder can experiment with alternate choices. If one solves for a given endogenous variable using the structural equation that explains it in the system (31), experience has shown that such a choice for (32) often leads to convergence.

Convergence of the Gauss-Seidel algorithm is also influenced by the selection of the initial values to use for the current endogenous variables in the first stage of the iterative solution procedure. These choices may be as critical in some cases as the way in which normalization choices are made. Generally, the closer the choices of the initial values are to the actual solution, the more rapidly the algorithm converges. More distant choices may lead to nonconvergence of the algorithm. Because the solutions are the forecasts that are being sought through the use of the model, convergence of the Gauss-Seidel algorithm implies that the model builder should choose initial values for the endogenous variables which are close to the actual forecasts to be produced by the model's structure.

24

Near-Triangular Rearrangements in Solving Nonlinear Systems

For the major econometric models the equations (32) can be arranged in a manner that permits considerable simplification, because a current endogenous variable is typically excluded from many of the structural equations of the system. The equations can be rearranged into three groups, each of which is in triangular form or near triangular form so that after rearrangement the entire system is as near to block recursive form as the nonlinearities permit.

The first of these groups of equations consists of those in which none of the current endogenous variables enter into the right-hand sides of (32); or, if other current endogenous variables are present on the right-hand sides of (32), the corresponding equations for these variables do not contain any current endogenous variables. Typically, equations will be found in this group for business fixed investment, residential construction, allowances for capital consumption, and capital stocks. Forecasted values of such current endogenous variables can be obtained directly from the values of the predetermined and exogenous variables without the use of special numerical methods when the equations (32) are available. Standard matrix inversion methods can be employed, or the equations can be rearranged into a triangular or recursive form and then solved.

The second group of equations consists of those current endogenous variables whose equations in (32) have at least one other current endogenous variable on the right-hand sides of (32), which cannot be forecasted solely from the predetermined and exogenous variables alone. In addition, each of these endogenous variables itself appears on the right-hand side of at least one other equation in (32) and therefore is simultaneously related to still other current endogenous variables of the system.

Ordering the equations in the second group into a triangular or near triangular form is more difficult than for the equations in the first group. The ordering of the second group is usually guided by a knowledge of economic relationships. For example, relationships between real and price sectors of the model are often utilized for this purpose. The real sector may consist of equations for endogenous expenditure components of gross national product other than business and residential investment, for industry outputs, employment, hours worked, gross national product, and various components of national income. The price sector may contain interest rates, wage rates, prices, demand and time deposits, and wage payments by sector (aggregate wage payments being in the real block).

Unfortunately, full triangularity may not be achieved because price variables depend on variables in the real sector as well as on those in the first group of equations, and variables in the real block depend on price variables as well as on variables in the first group. Even when the most favorable ordering has been accomplished, the simultaneous relationships may be so complex that this ordering does not produce a near block recursive form for the second group of variables. Because the Gauss-Seidel algorithm is applied essentially to the equations in the second group, the manner in which equations are ordered and variables are classified between the real and price sectors has important implications for the convergence of the Gauss-Seidel algorithm.

Application of the Gauss-Seidel algorithm to this group of equations requires specification of the initial values of the variables being solved for in the real and price sectors. Because the second group is not in triangular form, when solving for variables in the price sector, the initial values of the variables in the real sector must be used together with the initial values of the variables in the price sector. Thus conditional solutions to the price sector variables are obtained, which depend on the initial values of the variables in the real sector. In turn, these conditional values from the price sector are used to solve for the variables in the real sector. Thus the real sector solutions are also conditional on the values from the price sector. This process of cycling conditional solutions between the price and real sectors is repeated, and the Gauss-Seidel algorithm is iterated until a sequence of conditional solutions converging to the actual simultaneous solutions (when they exist) of the real and price sectors appears to be achieved.

The Gauss-Seidel algorithm, of course, does not converge for all initial values that might be assigned to the variables. Moreover, different orderings of the equations require different initial values to be specified for different sets of endogenous variables. Thus whether or not a solution is obtained for a model has been found to be influenced to a great extent by the ordering of the equations in the second group employed by the model builder. Sometimes changing the ordering of equations will not produce convergence, and an equation must be replaced by an alternate equation in order to obtain convergence.

Finally, the Gauss-Seidel algorithm is frequently modified beyond the reordering of equations and the substitution of alternate equations by employing a simultaneous overrelaxation procedure, which is sometimes referred to as *damping*. This procedure usually consists of the application of appropriately selected weights that assist convergence.

The third group of endogenous variables are those for which

equations in (32) have at least one other current endogenous variable on the right-hand side of (32) that cannot be forecasted solely from the predetermined and endogenous variables, but which themselves are not simultaneously related as explanatory variables (although they may appear as lagged endogenous variables in other equations). Such variables are typically profits and entrepreneurial income by sector. Forecasts for these variables are also obtained directly without the use of special methods when the values of the required endogenous variables in the first and second groups are determined as discussed above.

A serious issue in the development and use of nonlinear econometric models for forecasting and policy analysis is the question of the existence of multiple solutions to the equation system (32). This problem is more difficult with nonlinear systems than with linear systems because we lack a general theory for characterizing the existence of zeros in nonlinear systems. When multiple solutions exist, it may be possible to discard some by appealing to economic theory. For example, one would discard a solution to a nonlinear model for which real wages would fall at negative unemployment rates. On the other hand, multiple solutions may exist, and each could have reasonable and valid economic interpretations which could lead to different forecasts and widely different policy assessments. Because model builders are aware of the implications of multiple solutions and because they lack a general analytical characterization for nonlinear systems, they routinely vary selected initial conditions and examine whether they lead to alternative solutions using the Gauss-Seidel algorithm. Although these heuristic procedures may be satisfactory for some nonlinearities, their use is often limited in practice because of computational costs and other factors. The actual status of multiple solutions remains unfathomed for nonlinear models, and their consequences, practical as well as theoretical, remain largely unexplored in forecasting and policy analysis. Increased acceptance and use of nonlinear models will depend in part on a more systematic and deeper investigation of multiple solutions and on a more satisfactory resolution of this issue than is currently available.

3

Studies of Forecast Errors
of Major Econometric Models

Previous Major Studies

Studies of the short-term forecast error performance of major econometric models began to appear in the literature in the 1960s. Since that time many studies have been made of the forecasts of different variables from different models and over various time periods. Forecast errors have been analyzed using a variety of approaches, and studies range from simple comparisons of descriptive measures of forecast errors by independent researchers to coordinated attempts at forecast evaluation and comparison by a group of the major model builders themselves.

Major studies by individuals are Zarnowitz [51, 52], Mincer and Zarnowitz [41], Hickman [27], Haitovsky, Treyz, and Su [25], and McNees [39]. In addition, at least three volumes of collected papers by various authors relating to the Brookings Econometric Model have appeared (Duesenberry et al. [13, 14], and Fromm and Klein [21]), each of which contain some discussion of the subject of forecast errors. An example of an investigation by a group of major model builders is the Model Comparison Study supported by the National Bureau of Economic Research and the National Science Foundation (NBER/NSF) which is discussed in the next section and in Chapter 6.

Five principal findings emerged from the studies of the independent researchers.

1. For a given model, ex ante forecasts, which are based on the econometrician's adjustments of constant terms in model equations and judgmentally determined values of exogenous and predetermined variables, often have smaller root mean squared errors (RSMEs) than do forecasts that are developed for the

same periods of time (using the same constant term adjustments) but that are based on the actual values of the exogenous and predetermined variables. The model builder's adjustments of the constant terms used in these forecasts, of course, are attempts to adjust for observed forecast error bias and serial correlation in the errors.

2. Ex post forecasts with or without constant term adjustments but with actual values of exogenous and predetermined variables often have RSMEs which have about the same magnitudes as the RSMEs calculated from forecasts based on naive time series models, which assume no change, or constant nonzero change, or constant percent change from period to period in the variable being forecasted.

3. Ex ante forecasts of major turning points by econometric models are unrealiable. Both the ex ante and ex post forecasting performances of econometric models are substantially poorer when made at the time of major turning points than at times of sustained expansion or contraction. Moreover, the RSMEs of forecast errors are larger when made for periods that turn out to contain a turning point.

4. Some variables are forecasted with smaller RSMEs over an expansionary period, while for other variables the reverse is true.

5. It appears that no one of the major econometric models forecasts a given variable better than other models for all periods extending through an expansion, a decline, and a subsequent expansion.

The McNees [39] study compared the errors of two largely noneconometric forecasts with ex ante forecast errors generated by a group of the major U.S. econometric models for the first half of the 1970s. The two noneconometric forecasts were from the surveys of about fifty forecasters made jointly by the American Statistical Association and the National Bureau of Economic Research and from the Mapcast Group of the General Electric Company. The ASA-NBER surveys consisted largely of the responses of business economists, eleven of whom had access to their own econometric models and about twenty-five of whom had access to an outsider's model. Only a few of the respondents, however, indicated that such a model was the primary method for developing their forecast. McNees used the median of the respondents' forecasts as the panel's forecast for a given quarter. The Mapcast Group at General Electric also used judgmental methods in developing its forecasts. McNees found, after analyzing forecast errors in a variety of ways, that forecasts "not based on formal econometric models appeared to be generally as accurate or more accurate than econometrically based forecasts" (p. 31). He concluded that "on the basis of the evidence presented here, the contribution of econometric models to forecasting accuracy can neither be established nor denied" (p. 34).

In a still more recent study, Zarnowitz [53], as part of the continuing NBER program of studies in forecasting behavior and performance, analyzed quarterly forecasts of the U.S. Department of Commerce's BEA model, the Wharton Mark III, Chase, and Data Resources, Inc. (DRI) models, as well as those of the GE Mapcast group and of the ASA-NBER panel of forecasters. The quarterly and annual forecast performances for 1970–1975 were investigated. Zarnowitz concludes, on the basis of an examination of various descriptive measures calculated from these forecasts, that forecasts of real growth and inflation tend to be poorer than forecasts of annual percentage change in nominal or current dollar GNP. Indeed, he gives "good marks for overall accuracy" to the econometric models' forecasts of such annual percentage changes, but he states that forecasts of real GNP growth suffer from large turning-point errors while inflation forecasts are characterized by large errors of underestimation. Over the period studied, output tends to be overestimated in times of low growth and underestimated in times of high growth. Although the econometric models' forecasts have a favorable record of predicting annual current dollar GNP, the same cannot be said of predicting quarterly changes in current dollar GNP within one year ahead or beyond one year. He concludes: "At the present time, the predictive value of detailed forecasts reaching out further than a few quarters ahead must be rather heavily discounted."

The NBER/NSF Model Comparison Study

A recent comprehensive study of forecast errors and policy multipliers was undertaken by the leading American econometric model builders who participated in the Model Comparison Seminar of the NBER/NSF Conference on Econometrics and Mathematical Economics. Fromm and Klein [20, 22] have presented summaries and overviews of the conference findings. More detailed discussions of these findings and related papers have been gathered into a book edited by Burmeister and Klein [8], who describe how the various papers contribute to the objective of providing a framework for analyzing forecasting performance and policy assessments of econometric models. The research extended over a three-year period, and the models included in the investigation were the BEA model, the Brookings model, the University of Michigan model, the DRI model, a model of R. C. Fair, the model of the Federal Reserve Bank of St. Louis, the MPS model (jointly supervised by persons from MIT and the University of Pennsylvania and partly supported by the Social Science Research Council), the Wharton Mark III model and its anticipations version, the Hickman-Coen annual model, the Wharton annual model, and the Liu-Hwa monthly model. All except the last three are quarterly models.

Fromm and Klein [22] observe that despite the many differences in the models, all have "strong similarities" except for the St. Louis model, which is referred to as a monetarist model. The remaining models employ a Keynesian type ISLM framework, in which expenditures depend on income and related variables, and income and production are expressed as functions of expenditures or factor costs. Notwithstanding these similarities, the models differ in important respects, including the choice of endogenous, exogenous, and predetermined variables as well as in the modeling of financial and real sector interactions.

With respect to forecast errors, simulated forecasts were developed by all participants for twenty macroeconomic variables. The Fromm and Klein [22] summary presents only RSME calculations for simulations within the sample period and for those made beyond the sample period for ex post forecasts. The latter are referred to as extrapolations. Constant term adjustments were made for the simulations in some, but not all, of the models.

The principal conclusions of this cooperative study of the major models are the following:

1. Considerable differences exist in the RSMEs between forecasts of different variables for a given model. For example, the RSMEs associated with business fixed investment and inventory investment are as large as those for aggregate consumption, although the latter is a far larger component of GNP than the former. On the income side, RSMEs for profits are as large as those associated with wages, though again wages are a much larger component of GNP than are profits. Also, simulations of the long-term interest rate have smaller RSMEs than do simulations of the short-term rate. In general, variables which are relatively stable over time are simulated with smaller RSMEs than are variables having large fluctuations from period to period.

TABLE 3

ROOT MEAN SQUARED ERRORS FOR CONSUMPTION EXPENDITURES

Model	Quarters Ahead for Extrapolation outside Sample Period							
	1	2	3	4	5	6	7	8
Nominal consumption								
BEA	4.61	9.12	13.41	16.20	18.46	20.09	—[a]	—[a]
Wharton Mark III	5.87	10.43	14.82	17.33	21.64	25.40	28.32	30.32
Real Consumption								
BEA	4.26	7.21	9.41	10.02	9.81	9.16	—[a]	—[a]
Wharton Mark III	2.89	5.04	7.21	8.51	9.31	9.25	8.53	6.97

[a] BEA model extrapolations are for six quarters only.
SOURCE: Fromm and Klein [22], table 3, p. 10.

2. Considerable differences exist between RSMEs for the same variable across models. Table 3 shows RSMEs for extrapolations beyond the sample period of nominal (or current) and real consumption expenditures for the BEA and Wharton Mark III models, and Table 4 shows RSMEs for extrapolations of nominal and

TABLE 4

ROOT MEAN SQUARED ERRORS FOR GROSS NATIONAL PRODUCT

Model	Quarters Ahead for Extrapolation outside Sample Period							
	1	2	3	4	5	6	7	8
Nominal GNP								
BEA	4.30	12.47	18.21	20.78	21.13	19.72	—[a]	—[a]
Wharton Mark III	5.71	17.04	25.09	27.25	34.13	40.35	43.99	46.57
Real GNP								
BEA	3.51	9.05	11.54	11.02	8.42	6.83	—[a]	—[a]
Wharton Mark III	5.02	12.96	17.96	19.35	21.24	21.55	19.73	17.03

[a] BEA model extrapolations are for six quarters only.
SOURCE: Fromm and Klein [22], table 2, p. 9.

real GNP for the same models. The differences between the RSMEs are readily observed.

3. RSMEs increase with the length of the forecast period. The RSME for the one-step-ahead forecast is smaller than for the two-steps-ahead forecast, and so on. There are, however, some exceptions to this generalization, and occasionally the RSMEs for the more distant steps-ahead forecasts are smaller than those for shorter-time horizons. This can be seen in Table 4, where the RSME for the eight-steps-ahead forecast for real GNP is smaller than that for the three-, four-, five-, and six-steps-ahead forecasts for the Wharton model, while the six-steps-ahead forecast for the BEA model is smaller than the two-, three-, four-, and five-steps-ahead forecasts.

4. Outside the sample period there appears to be an important bias in the simulation forecasts of the levels of variables such as real and nominal GNP. This bias does not appear to be present in the extrapolations of the first differences of the same variables.

5. For a given variable, the RSMEs associated with postsample simulations often are two to three times larger than the RSMEs for the simulations within the sample period. Fromm and Klein assert that postsample simulation error is "just on the borderline of being usable for policy application. There is definitely room for improvement although empirical models with this observed degree of imprecision have proved to be useful in decision-making processes" (p. 5).

In order to obtain comparable simulation results both within and outside the sample period, the model proprietors attempted to standardize the important features of their exercise. They were to choose the same sample period (1961–1969), the same extrapolation period, the same number of steps ahead in the forecast horizon, the same initial conditions for all models at the beginning of the sample period, and the same initial conditions for all models at the beginning of the extrapolation period. The same variables were to be chosen to be forecasted. Finally, the simulated forecast errors were to be summarized by calculating the root mean square errors.

Unfortunately, these standards of uniformity were not achieved in the work of the seminar. It was not possible to choose the same sample period for each model. In fact, only the two versions of the Wharton Mark III model had the same extrapolation periods and presumably the same sample periods. All the remaining models had different forecast extrapolation periods, and therefore it is likely that they had different sample periods as well. The discussion in Fromm and Klein on the choice of the sample periods is not clear on this important point, and the wide differences, to the extent that they can be identified from this paper, are shown in Table 5. Moreover, the number of steps ahead in the forecast horizon were not the same across models. Some models developed forecast simulations up to four steps ahead, while others had forecasts up to five, six, or eight steps ahead. Some of the models provided no extrapolations at all. These differences should be kept in mind when examining the RSMEs presented in Fromm and Klein [22].

In addition to these differences in the nature of the exercises performed by the participating model proprietors, one should keep in mind the difficulties relating to econometric model comparisons discussed in Chapters 1 and 2—namely, the different levels of aggregation in models, the different choices of exogenous and endogenous variables, the different lag structures that can be chosen even when the choices of the exogenous and endogenous variables are the same, and so on. A carefully developed experimental design and a sound statistical analysis of results dealing effectively with these more serious difficulties relating to model structure are needed, as well as successful standardization of conditions under which computer simu-

TABLE 5

SAMPLE AND FORECAST EXTRAPOLATION PERIODS OF THE NBER/NSF
MODEL COMPARISON SEMINAR

Model	Sample Period	Extrapolation Period
BEA	Not given	1969.1–1971.2
Brookings	1959.1–1965.4	1966.1–1970.4
University of Michigan Model	Not given	1968.1–1970.4
DRI	1962.1–1968.4	No extrapolations given
Fair	1962.1–1967.4	1965.4–1969.4
St. Louis	Not given	1970.1–1971.4
MPS	Not given	Not given
Wharton Mark III	Not given	1970.2–1972.4
Wharton Anticipations Model	Not given	1970.2–1972.4
Hickman-Coen Annual	Not given	No extrapolations given
Wharton Annual	1961.01–1967.12	No extrapolations given
Liu-Hwa Monthly	1961–1967	1972.01–1972.12

SOURCE: Fromm and Klein [22], table 2, p. 9.

35

lation experiments are to be executed, before reliable comparisons of econometric model performance can be made.

In the light of these many difficulties in evaluating and comparing the forecasting performance and policy analysis capabilities of large-scale econometric models based on ex post simulations, the following assessment (Fromm and Klein [22], p. 4) of the design and work of the model comparison seminar may be less self-critical than is appropriate: "As a study group we set out with high standards for uniformity; but, as in any practical application, we had to allow many compromises. In the end we achieved about as much uniformity as we could hope to get from 12 teams of independent scholars—especially in economics."

It is clear that there are attractive features of a comparative ex post type of simulation study executed by a large group of different but cooperating model-building teams. Three major difficulties in any such study, however, may neutralize these attractions or eliminate them altogether. First, great difficulties are inevitably encountered in standardizing and controlling the conditions under which different groups of researchers are to perform comparative simulations. Second, a complex experimental design must be developed and implemented so that it is possible to examine adequately the effects of structural differences between various models on forecast errors. Third, a statistical analysis of the results of such experiments—even when they meet the criteria of standardized conditions and adequate experimental design—would involve making inferences from small samples of correlated forecast errors (as indicated in Chapter 5), and exact small-sample results are not available for a general statistical treatment of such sample data. For these reasons we believe that large-scale comparative studies based only on within-sample and postsample ex post simulations cannot lead to an entirely satisfactory resolution of the problem of comparing the forecasting performance of different models nor of individual models. Such studies should be complemented by examinations of ex ante forecast performance.

A principal difference between actual ex ante forecast errors and ex post simulations is that in making ex ante forecasts the model builders do not use actual values of the exogenous and predetermined variables of the system, because at the time the forecast is prepared such values are not available to the forecaster for future periods. Their values must be developed from judgmental considerations or from other forecasting models, sometimes called "hidden models," or from a combination of these. Another major difference is that the ex ante forecasts that are released by the model builders are not necessarily those produced directly by the models using forecasted or subjectively determined values of the exogenous variables (with or without constant term adjustments). In many cases these forecasts have been altered further by model builders in an ad hoc manner which reflects still other judgmental considerations. Thus actual ex ante forecasts result from considerable interaction of forecasters with their models. Because these forecasts are disseminated by the model proprietors and purchased by their clients, their properties are of great interest to their users. Analysis of ex ante errors is limited, however, in that one cannot allocate the forecast error explicitly to its various sources such as the model's structure, the specification of its exogenous variables, and the forecaster's judgmental inputs.

4

A Study of Ex Ante Forecast Errors of the Wharton, DRI, Chase, and BEA Quarterly Econometric Models

The Data Base

In this chapter we present an alternative descriptive analysis of forecast performance based on our own research. For this purpose we used actual ex ante forecasts of four major econometric models, the Data Resources, Inc. (DRI) model, the BEA model of the U.S. Department of Commerce, the Chase Econometric Associates model, and the Wharton Mark III model. The forecast errors were calculated from ex ante forecasts actually disseminated by the corresponding model proprietors. Although these forecasts resulted from the interaction of forecasters with their models in ways described earlier, we will refer to them simply as model forecasts and the errors of such forecasts as model errors.

Our study included analysis of forecasts of ten macroeconomic variables: current dollar or nominal GNP, GNP in 1958 dollars, implicit GNP price deflator in 1958 dollars, nonresidential fixed investment, residential fixed investment, change in business inventories, personal consumption expenditures on durable goods, personal consumption expenditures on nondurable goods and services, net exports, and unemployment rate. For convenience in exposition only selected results are presented here.

Throughout this discussion we have used the adjusted or revised forecast errors so as to take account of data revisions in the conventional way. The adjusted error for the τ-period-ahead forecast made at time t is

$$e_{t+\tau} = F_{t+\tau}^r - A_{t+\tau}^r = (A_t^r - A_t^u + F_{t+\tau}^u) - A_{t+\tau}^r$$

where A^r and A^u denote the revised and unrevised actual values of the variable considered, and F^r and F^u denote the revised and unre-

39

vised forecasts of this variable. In this study the unrevised actual values were those available in the fall of 1976 with two exceptions: The GNP implicit price deflator was expressed in terms of a 1958 base, as available prior to the major revisions of 1974. This deflator was then used to adjust the current dollar GNP (as of fall 1976) to obtain a constant dollar GNP having a 1958 base.

Forecasts for the DRI, Chase, and Wharton models are for a forecast horizon of one through eight quarters ahead, and forecasts for the BEA model are for one through five quarters ahead. Forecasts were made for the quarters 1970.3 through 1975.2. A set of one-through eight-steps-ahead forecasts for a given model is made from a specific quarter, which we call their base. As the base advances, new data are used to produce the next set of one- through eight-steps-ahead forecasts. In this sense the members of the forecast sets have a shifting base.

Descriptive Statistics of Ex Ante Forecast Errors

This discussion of forecast errors goes beyond that in the literature, which has consisted mainly of the presentation and analysis of simple averages, such as root mean square errors and mean absolute errors, or of other simple statistics such as the Theil U-statistic (see for example Fromm and Klein [22], Christ [9], Hirsch, Grimm, and Narasimham[28]). As alternatives to these simple statistics we present *descriptive* analyses of the forecast error data set which use methods from exploratory data analysis and some order statistics.

Table 6 shows various descriptive measures of the one- through eight-steps-ahead forecast errors of the DRI model for GNP in current dollars. Similar measures for the remaining forecast models for current dollar GNP are shown in Appendix Tables A1 to A3. These tables are largely self-explanatory; they display the maximum forecast error, the upper quartile or seventy-fifth percentile, the median, the lower quartile or twenty-fifth percentile, the minimum forecast error, the number of observations or forecast errors for the indicated step ahead of the forecast, the midspread or interquartile range (the midspread covers the middle 50 percent of the observations), the mean, and the standard deviation.

Many of these descriptive measures are conveniently displayed graphically by the use of box plots, which reveal central tendency and spread behavior as well as turning-point behavior associated with the forecast error data. Figure 1 shows box plots of the one- through eight-steps-ahead forecast errors for the DRI model for current dollar

TABLE 6

The DRI Model: Descriptive Measures of Forecast Errors for GNP in Current Dollars

Number of Steps Ahead	Maximum Forecast Error	Upper Quartile	Median	Lower Quartile	Minimum Forecast Error	Number of Observations	Midspread[a]	Mean	Standard Deviation
1	13.700	3.250	0.800	−9.150	−15.100	20	12.400	−1.335	8.106
2	41.000	12.400	−3.700	−8.400	−25.300	19	20.800	0.326	14.747
3	58.800	−3.400	−8.800	−12.600	−25.400	18	9.200	−1.911	23.317
4	76.500	−7.100	−13.200	−18.500	−33.000	17	11.400	−4.753	30.111
5	78.900	−10.850	−17.450	−25.350	−42.300	16	14.500	−9.431	32.044
6	54.300	−15.300	−22.800	−33.200	−38.700	15	17.900	−16.607	24.926
7	21.200	−26.400	−33.650	−35.500	−36.300	14	9.100	−25.171	18.895
8	8.900	−29.000	−36.100	−42.800	−53.900	13	13.800	−31.023	18.873

[a] The interquartile range, covering the middle 50 percent of the observations.
Source: Calculated from data provided by model builders.

FIGURE 1

THE DRI MODEL: BOX PLOTS OF FORECAST ERRORS FOR GNP IN CURRENT DOLLARS

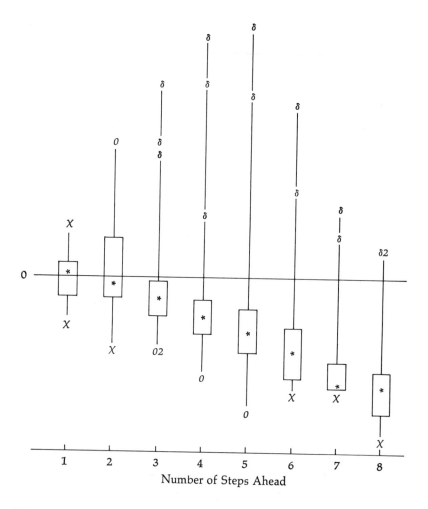

Number of Steps Ahead

GNP. Figures A1 through A3 in the Appendix display corresponding box plots for the remaining models.

The box plots conform to several conventions developed by Tukey [49]. The median is indicated by an asterisk, the lower and upper limits of a box, called hinges, are the twenty-fifth percentile or lower quartile and the seventy-fifth percentile or upper quartile, respectively. The difference between the lower and upper hinges is the interquartile range or midspread. A vertical line segment extends from

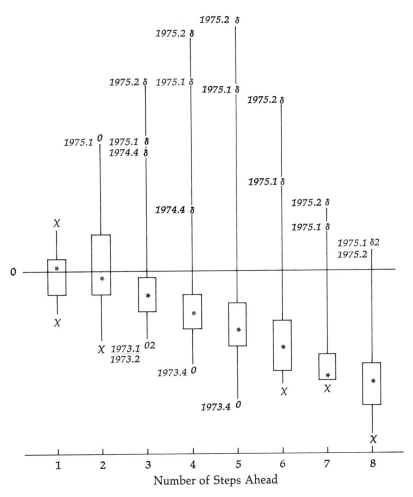

FIGURE 2

THE DRI MODEL: BOX PLOTS OF FORECAST ERRORS FOR GNP IN
CURRENT DOLLARS, WITH EXTREMES DATED

a hinge to the maximum or minimum (extreme) value of the corresponding errors. If an extreme is less than one interquartile distance
from a corresponding hinge, the vertical segment terminates with the
symbol X. If an extreme is between 1 and 1.5 times the midspread,
the line segment terminates with the symbol 0. If an extreme is greater
than 1.5 times the midspread, the terminating symbol is δ. All observations beyond one interquartile distance of a hinge are indicated so
that a visual impression of the extent of the data for each of the

43

FIGURE 3
Three-Steps-Ahead Forecasts of GNP Made by the DRI Model and Actual GNP

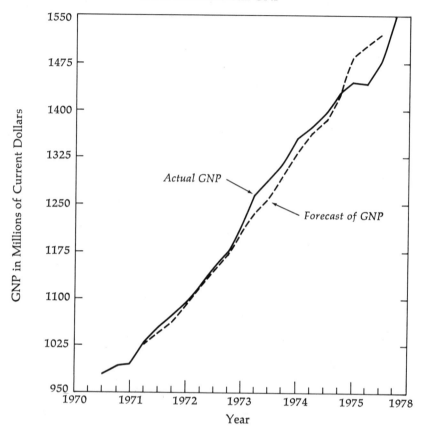

steps ahead of the forecast can be quickly formed. When several extreme forecast errors are so close to each other that they cannot be printed separately by the plotting device, one symbol appears followed by the number of such extremes. For example, in Figure 1 there are two extreme underforecasting errors for the three-steps-ahead forecasts which are nearly equal. Box plots are presented for only one of the ten variables studied, GNP in current dollars.

The forecast error is defined as the forecasted value minus the actual value; thus a negative error indicates that the forecast is smaller than the actual value or that underforecasting has occurred, and a positive error indicates that the forecast is greater than the actual value or that overforecasting has occurred. A zero line is drawn on

FIGURE 4

BOX PLOTS OF ONE-STEP-AHEAD FORECAST ERRORS FOR GNP IN
CURRENT DOLLARS FOR FOUR MODELS

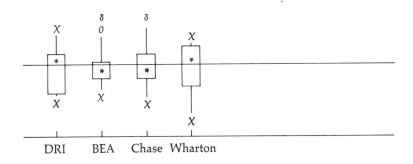

DRI   BEA   Chase Wharton

the box plots for ease of reference. An examination of the figure and corresponding table indicates that the median of the forecast errors is negative in all cases except two. There is a pronounced downward drift in the medians, suggesting a persistent tendency in these data toward underforecasting of GNP in current dollars. Similar patterns were observed in the box plots for other variables (see Appendix). At the same time, each of the models displays a tendency to produce a few forecasts which result from overforecasting by large amounts.

Box plots can be useful for examining turning-point performance of forecasting models. In Figure 2, for example, the large errors (those which are one or more times the interquartile distance from a hinge) are identified by the quarter to which the error refers. Large overforecasting errors occurred for the fourth quarter of 1974 and for the first and second quarters of 1975. For example, GNP in current dollars for 1975.1 was seriously overforecasted successively in the two-through eight-steps-ahead forecasts for this quarter (that is, for the eight-steps-ahead forecast for 1975.1 made in 1973.1 and continuing successively for each quarter through the two-steps-ahead forecast for 1975.1 made in 1974.3). Figure 3 shows actual GNP in current dollars for 1970.2 through 1975.3, together with the three-steps-ahead forecasts made by the DRI model for the quarters shown. The overforecasting extremes of the box plots in Figure 2 for the three-steps-ahead forecasts can also be seen from Figure 3 to be associated with turning points. The period from 1974.4 to 1975.1 was part of a severe recession, in which a decline of 6.6 percent in real GNP occurred over the period 1973.4 through 1975.1. Nominal GNP first began to decline in 1974.4, however.

FIGURE 5

BOX PLOTS OF THREE-STEPS-AHEAD FORECAST ERRORS FOR GNP IN
CURRENT DOLLARS FOR FOUR MODELS

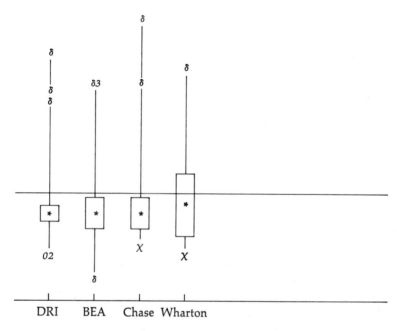

Underforecasting, but by relatively smaller amounts, occurred in
the three-steps-ahead forecasts made for 1973.1 and 1973.2. The
underforecasting extremes are also shown in Figure 3 for the three-
steps-ahead forecasts. This was a period of rapid acceleration in prices
as a result of sharp increases in demand for output and repercussions
from world commodity price movements and the oil embargo.

Figure 4 shows box plots of one-step-ahead forecast errors for
each of the four models, and Figure 5 shows box plots for each of the
models for the three-steps-ahead forecast errors. From these figures
one can easily see how the one- and three-steps-ahead forecast errors
vary across the models shown. Box plots for all models for the remaining steps ahead for current dollar GNP are shown in Figures A1
through A9 in the Appendix.

5

Major Issues of Statistical Inference in Analyzing Forecasting Performance

Limitations of Descriptive Measures

Although one can rank models in terms of forecast error performance by using one or more descriptive measures, such as means, midspreads, and root mean squared errors, such ranking relates only to the specific time period of the data set used. It can and usually does change when different time periods are selected for study or when other variables are investigated. It is impossible to determine with a high degree of confidence which econometric model will forecast a given variable best in the future on the basis of descriptive measures of past forecast performance. The reason for this is that the evaluation of the forecast error performance of models is properly a problem of statistical inferences concerning parameters of distributions of forecast errors over time. Because such statistical inferences must take account of correlations among the errors for a given model as well as across models, they are exceedingly difficult to make even if long forecast histories are available. In short, because of the extensive correlation structure, one can pass from descriptive measures to inferences concerning forecast performance only with great difficulty. All studies of the forecasting performance of the major econometric models known to the authors have failed to state this problem explicitly and to treat it adequately. They must therefore be considered only as descriptive analyses of model forecasting performance for given variables and for specific time periods. For a smaller model, Fair [17] has attempted to estimate standard errors of forecast. Fair's model has 95 equations, of which only 28 are stochastic. The model has 180 coefficients (including 14 serial correlation coefficients) which must be estimated from data. His standard errors were estimated from approximately

FIGURE 6

SOME OF THE CORRELATION STRUCTURE OF FORECAST ERRORS
OF AN ECONOMETRIC MODEL

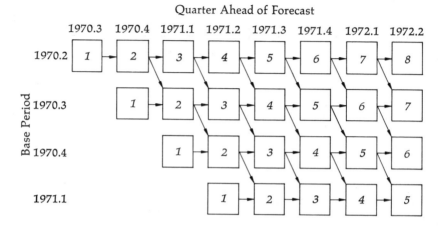

3,300 simulation trials of his model, rather than from the use of the actual standard error of the underlying exact sampling distribution of errors.

Correlation Structure of Forecast Errors and Statistical Inference

Figure 6 illustrates part of the correlation structure for a forecast error data set and for a given model in the study. Each arrow in the figure indicates a correlation. The first row indicates one- through eight-steps-ahead forecasts made from a base period of 1970.2, the second row shows one- through seven-quarters-ahead forecasts made from a base period of 1970.3, and so forth. Diagonal arrows indicate correlations between corresponding τ-step-ahead forecasts made from different base periods. Lateral arrows for a given row indicate correlations existing across forecasts made from a common base period. Still other correlations are present which are not indicated in the figure, and there could be, in addition, cross-correlation effects in forecast errors between models.

In a recent study, Ansley, Spivey, and Wrobleski [3] examined correlations for the errors in the one-step-ahead forecasts of changes in levels of nominal gross national product, unemployment rate, and investment in residential structures for the BEA and DRI models, using data for the same time period as that used in Chapter 4. Although one might expect no correlation in the one-step-ahead forecast errors, the authors found evidence of positive serial correlation even in these errors, using the von Neumann test statistic for first order serial correlation at the 10 percent level of significance. In addition, the one-step-ahead forecast errors between the BEA and DRI models were examined in terms of the simple, contemporaneous cross-correlations. Again, at the 10 percent level, significant correlations were found for the forecast errors of the three variables for these models. Although the structures of the DRI and BEA models differ in many important respects—different sizes of equation systems, different choices of exogenous and endogenous variables, and different lag structures—it was nevertheless concluded that the one-step-ahead forecast errors for the same variables from the different models are correlated.

If we can make the assumption that such forecast errors are covariance stationary processes, then the estimation of the covariance structure of these processes could be carried out in two ways. One would be to use the standard asymptotic results associated with autocorrelation and cross-correlation structures either for time or for frequency domains. Alternatively, one could exploit the Wold decomposition and model the forecast errors as multivariate moving average processes and then estimate the parameters of these processes through appropriate large sample methods. These estimators could then be used to estimate the covariance structure. Neither of these approaches is generally available, however, because of the small size of the forecast error data bases available at present. For example, for a given econometric model whose errors are in the data base of this study, there are nineteen correlated two-steps-ahead forecasts and, finally, thirteen correlated eight-steps-ahead forecasts. Moreover, there are only thirteen replications of complete sets of one- through eight-steps-ahead forecasts for each model, and these are themselves correlated. For these reasons, attempts at parametric estimation of the complete correlation structure by either of the methods mentioned above would lead to results which have unsatisfactory small-sample properties. Estimators would have low precision, and tests of hypotheses would have low power. Thus statistical inferences that would lead to useful discriminations between models on the basis of forecast error performance cannot be made at present.

Major studies of forecast errors of econometric models (Fromm and Klein [22], Christ [9], Haitovsky, Treyz, and Su [25], Hirsch, Grimm, and Narasimham [28], McNees [39], Mincer and Zarnowitz [41], and Zarnowitz [52, 53], for example) have featured tables of root mean squares or of mean absolute deviations, which were calculated from errors having correlation structures similar to those illustrated in Figure 6. These studies can be interpreted only as descriptive analyses which relate to specific data sets and time periods; they do not provide a basis for statistical inferences for comparing model forecasting performance. In particular, descriptive measures such as root mean squares do not yield reliable statistical inferences because they are calculated from small sets of observations that are realizations of stochastic processes having complicated correlation structures.

This inconclusive state of affairs will continue until forecast error data sets for longer periods of time are made available by model proprietors. One helpful approach would be for model proprietors to make the past one- through eight-steps-ahead forecasts for a current quarter regularly available to independent researchers. Sharing this information would not reduce the value to clients of information contained in forecasts for future quarters whose base is the current quarter.

6

Policy Multiplier Studies of Major Econometric Models

Policy Assessments Using Generalized Multipliers

The impact, interim, and total or cumulated multipliers developed in Chapter 1 were for linear econometric models in which the reduced form had only one-period lags, as in equation (14). Analytical expressions for these multipliers were developed which give the effects of policy changes on the endogenous variables when these changes are restricted to a single variable. Practically speaking, methods of policy assessment should be sufficiently flexible so that changes of differing amounts in several variables could be examined simultaneously. Moreover, these methods should provide assessments of the effects of policy changes extending over time periods of differing lengths, with some changes sustained for long periods and others for a short time only.

Explicit analytical formulas expressing the effects of these more general policy assessments are not presented in standard econometrics textbooks and would be extremely difficult to determine, even for linear models. For large nonlinear models, explicit multiplier expressions are not available even for policy changes restricted to one variable. Therefore it has been suggested by Klein [36] and others that a generalized multiplier concept be employed which utilizes the system (32) and the Gauss-Seidel alogrithm to determine families of solutions under alternate specifications of policy changes.

The first step in developing generalized policy multipliers is to calculate a *control solution* (prediction or forecast) from the model for a sequence of time periods embracing the horizon of the policy assessment to be made. This horizon is often considerably longer than that used in standard short-term forecasting, and thus multiplier calculations require judgmental considerations beyond those ordinarily employed in developing a short-term forecast. These calculations can be either ex ante or ex post and either within or outside the sample period.

As in short-term forecasting, a control solution requires the specification of exogenous and predetermined variables over the policy horizon, including the policy variables which are to be changed and whose effects are to be examined. Specification of all these variables must be made for the longer time horizon in a manner consistent with that for the short-term forecast period. In addition, values of the variables must be compatible with the fixed behavioral relationships used in the policy assessment. The control solution for the jth endogenous variable and for the periods $t+1, \cdots, t+h$ of the policy horizon is denoted

$$(33) \qquad \hat{y}_j^{(c)}(t+1), \cdots, \hat{y}_j^{(c)}(t+h).$$

In the second step an alternative solution corresponding to the prescribed changes in the policy being examined is then calculated from (32) in a manner analogous to that of the control solution. This requires further judgmental considerations relating to the consistency over the policy horizon of the selected values of the exogenous and predetermined variables with the specification of the changes in the policy variables. This gives for the jth endogenous variable an alternative solution path of the model over the chosen time horizon of the policy analysis,

$$(34) \qquad \hat{y}_j^{(a)}(t+1), \cdots, \hat{y}_j^{(a)}(t+h).$$

A comparison of the two solutions (33) and (34)—or what can be called a comparison of the two time paths of dynamic solutions—generalizes the multiplier concepts presented earlier for the linear model. For example, when the policy change takes the form of a constant increment in one of the predetermined or exogenous policy variables, say,

$$(35) \qquad \Delta_j = x_j^{(a)}(t+k) - x_j^{(c)}(t+k) \qquad k = 1, \cdots, h,$$

then the generalized dynamic multiplier for the jth endogenous variable in the kth period can be defined as

$$(36) \qquad \frac{\hat{y}_j^{(a)}(t+k) - \hat{y}_j^{(c)}(t+k)}{\Delta_j} \qquad k = 1, \cdots, h.$$

The locus of these values portrays the generalized dynamic multiplier path of the nonlinear econometric model with respect to the given policy change.

In this context we see that a generalized multiplier involves the

52

calculation of alternate predictions which are special types of long-run forecasts. From an analytical point of view, these multipliers are mathematical functionals of what we have called predictions. Because predictions are random variables, such multipliers are random functionals over an appropriate Hilbert-type probability space. Therefore the study of generalized multipliers is intimately related to the study of random functionals and their inference properties. Moreover, another important aspect of the study of generalized multipliers is their relationship to the problem of prediction under structural economic relationships that are assumed to be unaffected by the policy changes whose long-run effects we are seeking to examine. We will return to the problem of structural change in the last section.

The NBER/NSF Model Comparison Study of Dynamic Policy Multipliers

The model comparison seminar also developed dynamic policy simulation studies in an attempt to evaluate model performance with respect to policy assessment. Common fiscal policy variables were changed, and the effects of these changes were studied with and without an accommodating monetary policy change. Fromm and Klein [22] presented tables relating to three dynamic multipliers: (1) change in GNP with respect to change in nondefense government expenditures; (2) change in GNP with respect to change in personal taxes; (3) change in GNP with respect to change in unborrowed reserves or money stock. Simulations were carried out for periods of up to ten years, with some quarterly models having extrapolation periods of forty quarters. The multipliers were presented in both current and real (1958) dollars, and the first multiplier indicated above was calculated with and without an accommodating monetary policy change.

Graphs of the multiplier results for the DRI, BEA, and Wharton Mark III models and the Wharton annual model appear in Figures 7 and 8. Figure 7 shows the policy multipliers estimating the effect on real GNP in 1958 dollars of a $1 billion increase in real governmental expenditures, which are maintained throughout the simulation period unaccompanied by an accommodating change in monetary policy. Figure 8 presents the dynamic multipliers representing the effects of a $1 billion increase in unborrowed reserves on real GNP in 1958 dollars. This $1 billion increase was also maintained throughout the simulation period.

Christ [9] attempted to analyze the multiplier data presented in Fromm and Klein [22], of which the data in Figures 7 and 8 are a

FIGURE 7

POLICY MULTIPLIERS FOR CHANGE IN REAL GNP (1958 DOLLARS) WITH RESPECT TO A MAINTAINED $1 BILLION INCREASE IN REAL GOVERNMENT EXPENDITURES WITHOUT ACCOMMODATIONS IN MONETARY POLICY

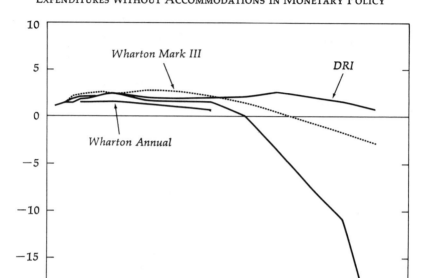

SOURCE: Fromm and Klein [22].

part, and concluded that "the models disagree very strongly about the effects that follow from important fiscal and monetary policy actions" (p. 72). Fromm and Klein, on the other hand, concluded that there is relatively uniform agreement across models with respect to the patterns and magnitudes of fiscal policy multipliers, while acknowledging the existence of "striking disparities" in multiplier responses to changes in monetary policy. As can be seen from Figure 7, all the models chosen for study displayed roughly similar fiscal multiplier paths for at least the first twenty quarters, with sharp differences appearing beyond twenty-four quarters. The multiplier paths in Figure 8, however, in which monetary policy effects appear, are dissimilar throughout.

Unfortunately, as with the NBER/NSF forecast error studies, the

FIGURE 8

POLICY MULTIPLIERS FOR CHANGE IN REAL GNP (1958 DOLLARS) FOR A
MAINTAINED $1 BILLION INCREASE IN UNBORROWED RESERVES

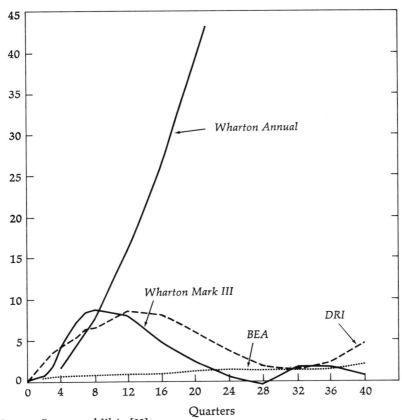

SOURCE: Fromm and Klein [22].

dynamic policy multiplier calculations were not carried out under uniform conditions. For example, the amounts of exogenous change in nondefense government expenditures varied from $5 billion in 1958 dollars to $1 billion in current dollars. Shifts in taxes and monetary policies also lacked uniformity across models, and policy simulation periods started at various times ranging from the beginning of recessions to the middle of expansionary periods. Moreover, because the models are nonlinear in variables, lack of uniformity in such critical conditions can produce further distortions in the dynamic multiplier paths beyond those attributable to such differences as the size of the models, exogeneity, and so on. Thus one can appreciate

55

the summary of these interpretational problems, given casually by Fromm and Klein: "lack of standardization hampers intermodel comparisons."

Structural Change in Assessing Policy Multipliers of Econometric Models

The relationship between the evaluation of policy multipliers and the short-run forecasting performance of econometric models must be kept in mind when examining multiplier paths such as those in Figures 7 and 8. As pointed out earlier, multipliers are merely special kinds of predictions developed from structural economic relationships that are usually assumed to be unaffected by the policy changes whose consequences are being examined. For example, if an econometric model produces unreliable short-run forecasts of major economic aggregates, it would be difficult to assign much credibility to its long-run multiplier calculations. Furthermore, as predictions, policy multipliers are estimates of unknown true multipliers. Such estimates, as pointed out in Chapter 5, are random variables, and statistical inferences concerning them require exact or asymptotic sampling distributions. Some asymptotic distribution results for estimates of impact and interim multipliers have been developed for linear structural models (Goldberger, Nagar, and Odeh [24], Schmidt [43], Brissimis and Gill [7]). However, exact small-sample results, which are most appropriate for the small data sets typically encountered in econometric practice, are not currently available even for linear models. In other words, for multipliers generated by large nonlinear econometric models, there are no exact or even asymptotic results that permit valid statistical inferences concerning the multiplier performance of the models. Nor do we have an appropriate inference framework for assessing whether the observed differences between multipliers of two or more models are large or small (that is, whether such differences are statistically significant). Specifically, the differences between the multipliers in Figure 7 for the first twenty quarters may be statistically significant although they may appear to be small visually. Alternatively, the larger discrepancies between multipliers observed in Figure 8 may not be statistically significant. Such statements of statistical significance require knowledge of the standard errors, which in turn depend on the sampling distributions whose central importance was indicated above.

Another dimension of this problem of assessing long-run multipliers is that the policy changes being examined may in turn produce changes over time in the structure of the economy. These may be expressed in an econometric model in a variety of ways. For example, the coefficients (parameters) of the econometric model can change over time as functions of either deterministic or stochastic drift. The variance-covariance matrix of the system can change, new variables may be introduced, or variables already in the model may change in relative importance. For example, if inflation rates, which have been approximately 2 to 3 percent, rise to sustained rates of 7 to 9 percent, this change may produce many shifts in relative prices and expectational processes in the economy which should be reflected in turn in the structural interrelationships between variables in an econometric model.

The statistical inferences associated with long-run policy multipliers in such situations should then be based not upon fixed parameter models (whether linear or nonlinear) but upon models whose properties also change through time. This problem, often called the problem of structural change, has been a subject of debate among both econometricians and economists. Some have advanced the view that econometric model forecasts for other than the short run (and hence all long-run multiplier calculations) are altogether unreliable because such structural changes necessarily accompany major policy changes. Lucas [38], p. 24, has developed this point of view in an emphatic fashion:

> I have argued simply that the standard, stable-parameter view of econometric theory and quantitative policy evaluation appears not to match several important characteristics of econometric practice, while an alternative general structure, embodying stochastic parameter drift, matches these characteristics very closely. This argument is, if accepted, sufficient to establish that the "long-run" implications of current forecasting models are without content, and that the short-term forecasting ability of these models provides no evidence of the accuracy to be expected from simulations of hypothetical policy rules.

With these complex basic research issues in mind it is difficult and perhaps impossible to resolve the differing assessments of Christ and of Fromm and Klein regarding the multiplier results of the NBER/NSF study. Much analytical work of a formidable character must be completed before choices can be made with confidence between econometric models on the basis of the assessment of multiplier performances.

APPENDIX

TABLE A1

THE BEA MODEL: DESCRIPTIVE MEASURES OF FORECAST ERRORS FOR GNP IN CURRENT DOLLARS

Number of Steps Ahead	Maximum Forecast Error	Upper Quartile	Median	Lower Quartile	Minimum Forecast Error	Number of Obser- vations	Midspread[a]	Mean	Standard Deviation
1	15.300	1.750	−2.200	−6.100	−10.300	20	7.850	−0.760	7.546
2	42.400	5.900	−1.300	−8.800	−22.800	19	14.700	0.453	14.580
3	44.400	−2.500	−6.650	−13.000	−32.900	18	10.500	−1.583	22.496
4	83.100	2.800	−10.600	−13.000	−29.700	17	15.800	−3.047	27.625
5	86.700	1.100	−10.550	−26.100	−46.500	16	27.200	−6.231	32.527

[a] The interquartile range, covering the middle 50 percent of the observations.
SOURCE: Calculated from data provided by model builders.

TABLE A2

THE CHASE MODEL: DESCRIPTIVE MEASURES OF FORECAST ERRORS FOR GNP IN CURRENT DOLLARS

Number of Steps Ahead	Maximum Forecast Error	Upper Quartile	Median	Lower Quartile	Minimum Forecast Error	Number of Observations	Midspread[a]	Mean	Standard Deviation
1	16.500	3.000	−0.100	−4.850	−14.400	20	7.850	−0.930	7.377
2	41.300	7.700	−5.400	−10.400	−23.700	19	18.100	−0.874	14.982
3	69.800	−0.900	−8.050	−14.100	−21.300	18	13.200	−1.822	23.310
4	73.500	−6.900	−11.800	−15.900	−26.800	17	9.000	−5.129	26.518
5	54.100	−12.600	−15.950	−23.600	−39.400	16	11.000	−12.119	23.266
6	35.700	−10.400	−29.800	−34.800	−36.600	15	24.400	−20.153	20.881
7	26.400	−27.300	−31.050	−45.000	−57.700	14	17.700	−28.857	22.737
8	23.000	−37.300	−43.200	−50.000	−59.700	13	12.700	−37.177	23.751

[a] The interquartile range, covering the middle 50 percent of the observations.
SOURCE: Calculated from data provided by model builders.

TABLE A3

The Wharton Model: Descriptive Measures of Forecast Errors for GNP in Current Dollars

Number of Steps Ahead	Maximum Forecast Error	Upper Quartile	Median	Lower Quartile	Minimum Forecast Error	Number of Observations	Midspread[a]	Mean	Standard Deviation
1	11.400	6.100	2.850	−7.150	−18.600	20	13.250	0.125	9.004
2	41.200	8.200	−0.600	−5.100	−27.100	19	13.300	1.237	14.220
3	51.400	7.900	−5.750	−17.400	−25.600	18	25.300	−1.133	20.747
4	65.800	1.600	−11.500	−20.000	−34.100	17	21.600	−4.332	25.861
5	63.400	−5.000	−17.650	−24.250	−51.400	16	19.250	−9.331	30.740
6	60.600	−12.100	−25.100	−37.700	−45.200	15	25.600	−18.630	28.628
7	20.500	−21.200	−33.600	−37.200	−60.100	14	16.000	−29.493	22.694
8	13.600	−28.100	−40.000	−55.000	−66.100	13	26.900	−36.746	24.676

[a] The interquartile range, covering the middle 50 percent of the observations.
Source: Calculated from data provided by model builders.

FIGURE A1
The BEA Model: Box Plots of Forecast Errors for GNP in Current Dollars

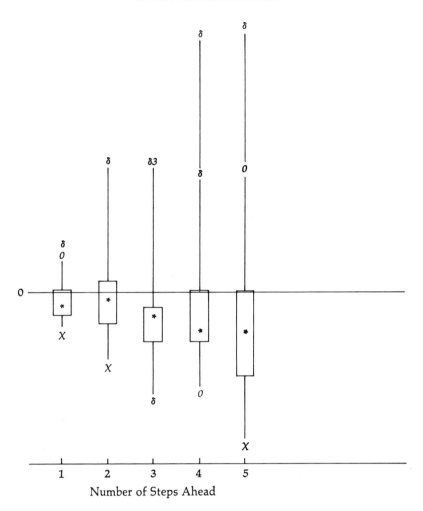

FIGURE A2
The Chase Model: Box Plots of Forecast Errors for GNP in Current Dollars

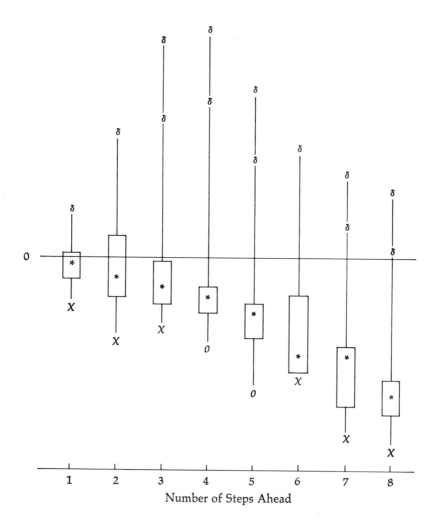

Number of Steps Ahead

FIGURE A3
The Wharton Model: Box Plots of Forecast Errors for GNP in Current Dollars

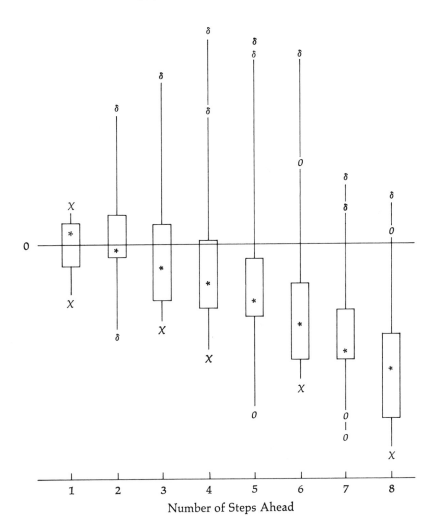

Number of Steps Ahead

FIGURE A4
Box Plots of Two-Steps-Ahead Forecast Errors for GNP in Current Dollars for Four Models

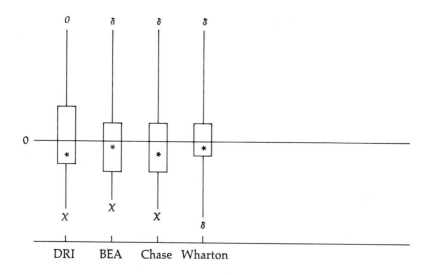

FIGURE A5
Box Plots of Four-Steps-Ahead Forecast Errors for GNP in Current Dollars for Four Models

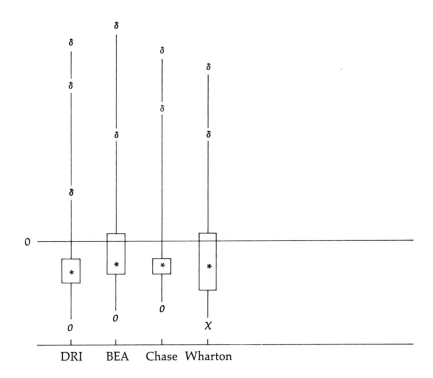

FIGURE A6
Box Plots of Five-Steps-Ahead Forecast Errors for GNP in Current Dollars for Four Models

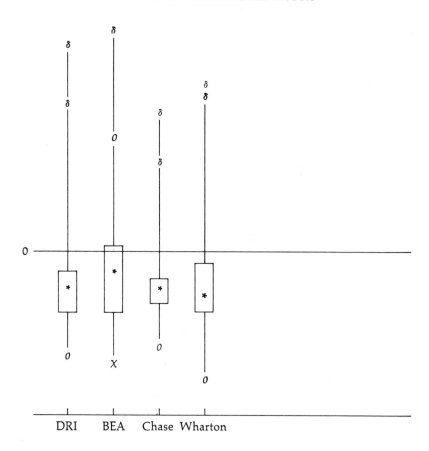

FIGURE A7
Box Plots of Six-Steps-Ahead Forecast Errors for GNP in Current Dollars for Three Models

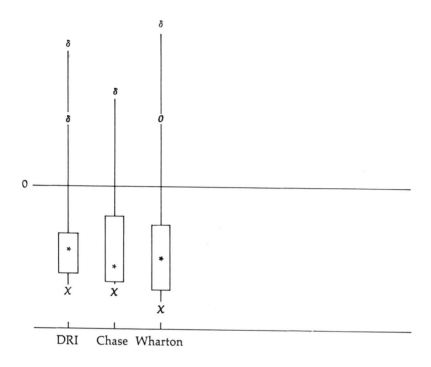

FIGURE A8
Box Plots of Seven-Steps-Ahead Forecast Errors for GNP in Current Dollars for Three Models

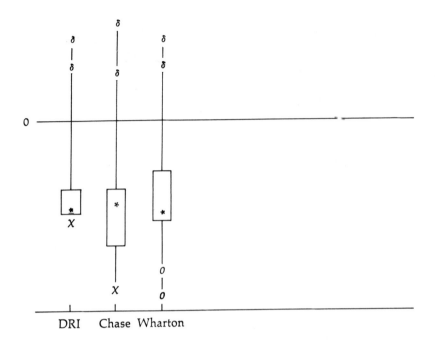

FIGURE A9
Box Plots of Eight-Steps-Ahead Forecast Errors for GNP in
Current Dollars for Three Models

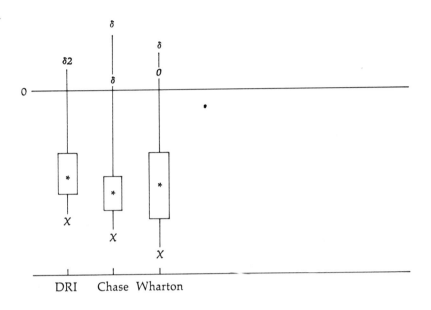

REFERENCES

1. Amemiya, T. "The Maximum Likelihood and the Nonlinear Three-Stage Least Squares Estimator in the General Nonlinear Simultaneous Equation Model." *Econometrica* 45 (1977): 955–968.

2. Anderson, T. W., and H. Rubin. "Estimation of the Parameters of a Single Equation in a Complete System of Stochastic Equations." *The Annals of Mathematical Statistics* 20 (1949): 46–63.

3. Ansley, C., W. A. Spivey, and W. J. Wrobleski. "Statistical Analysis of Forecast Errors of Econometric Models." *Proceedings of the American Statistical Association*, Business and Economic Statistics Section. 1978, pp. 203–207.

4. Basmann, R. L. "A Generalized Classical Method of Linear Estimation of Coefficients in a Structural Equation." *Econometrica* 25 (January 1957): 77–83.

5. Berndt, E., B. Hall, R. Hall, and J. A. Hausman. "Estimation and Inference in Nonlinear Structural Models." *Annals of Economic and Social Measurement* 3 (1974): 653–666.

6. Brissimis, S. N. "Multiplier Effects for Higher than First Order Linear Dynamic Econometric Models." *Econometrica* 44 (1976): 593–595.

7. Brissimis, S., and L. Gill. "On the Asymptotic Distribution of Impact and Interim Multipliers." *Econometrica* 46 (March 1978): 463–469.

8. Burmeister, E., and L. Klein, eds. *Econometric Model Performance*. Philadelphia: University of Pennsylvania Press, 1976.

9. Christ, C. "Judging the Performance of Econometric Models of the U.S. Economy." *International Economic Review* 16 (1975): 54–74.

10. Dhrymes, P. J. *Econometrics, Statistical Foundations and Applications*. New York: Harper and Row, 1970.

11. Dhrymes, P. J. *Distributed Lags: Problems of Estimation and Formulation*. San Francisco: Holden-Day, 1971.

12. Dhrymes, P. J., et al. "Criteria for Evaluation of Econometric Models." *Annals of Economic and Social Measurement* 1 (1972): 291–324.

13. Duesenberry, J., G. Fromm, L. Klein, and E. Kuh, eds. *The Brookings Quarterly Econometric Model of the United States*. Chicago: Rand McNally, 1965.

14. Duesenberry, J., et al., eds. *The Brookings Model: Some Further Results*. Chicago: Rand McNally, 1969.

15. Faddeeva, F. V. *Computational Methods of Linear Algebra*. New York: Dover Publications, 1959.

16. Fair, R. C. "An Evaluation of a Short-Run Forecasting Model." *International Economic Review* 15 (1974): 285–304.

17. Fair, R. C. "Estimating the Expected Predictive Accuracy of Econometric Models." Cowles Foundation Discussion Paper no. 480. Cowles Foundation for Research in Economics, Yale University, January 17, 1978.

18. Fisher, F. M. "Dynamic Structure and Estimation in Economywide Econometric Models." In Duesenberry [13], pp. 589–636.

19. Fisher, F. M. *The Identification Problem in Econometrics*. New York: McGraw-Hill, 1966.

20. Fromm, G., and L. Klein. "A Comparison of Eleven Econometric Models of the United States." *American Economic Review* 63 (1973): 385–393.

21. Fromm, G., and L. Klein, eds. *The Brookings Model: Perspective and Recent Developments*. New York: American Elsevier, 1975.

22. Fromm, G., and L. Klein. "The NBER/NSF Model Comparison Seminar: An Analysis of Results." *Annals of Economic and Social Measurement* 5 (1976): 1–27.

23. Fromm, G., and P. Taubman. *Policy Simulations with an Econometric Model*. Amsterdam: North Holland, 1967.

24. Goldberger, A. S., A. Nagar, and H. S. Odeh. "The Covariance Matrices of Reduced Form Coefficients and Forecasts for a Structural Econometric Model." *Econometrica* 29 (1961): 556–573.

25. Haitovsky, Y., G. Treyz, and V. Su. *Forecasts with Quarterly Macroeconometric Models*. New York: National Bureau of Economic Research, 1974.

26. Heien, D., J. Matthews, and A. Womack. "A Methods Note on the Gauss-Seidel Algorithm for Solving Econometric Models." *Agricultural Economics Research* 25, no. 3 (July 1973): 71–80.

27. Hickman, B. G., ed. *Econometric Models of Cyclical Behavior*. Vols. 1 and 2. New York: Columbia University Press, 1972.

28. Hirsch, A. A., B. Grimm, and G. V. L. Narasimham. "Some Multiplier and Error Characteristics of the BEA Model." *International Economic Review* 15 (1974): 616–631.

29. Howrey, E. P. "Dynamic Properties of a Condensed Version of the Wharton Model." In Hickman [27], pp. 601–662.

30. Hymans, S., and H. Shapiro. "The Structure and Properties of the Michigan Quarterly Econometric Model of the U.S. Economy." *International Economic Review* 15 (1974): 632–653.

31. Intrilligator, M. *Econometric Models, Techniques, and Applications*. Englewood Cliffs, N.J.: Prentice-Hall, 1978.

32. Johnston, J. *Econometric Methods*. 2d ed. New York: McGraw-Hill, 1972.

33. Jorgenson, D. W. "Rational Distributed Lag Functions." *Econometrica* 34 (1966): 135–149.

34. Jorgenson, D. W., and J. Laffont. "Efficient Estimation of Nonlinear Simultaneous Equations with Additive Disturbances." *Annals of Economic and Social Measurement* 3 (1974): 615–640.

35. Klein, L. R. *A Textbook of Econometrics*. 2d ed. Englewood Cliffs, N.J.: Prentice-Hall, 1974.

36. Klein, L. *An Essay on the Theory of Economic Prediction*. Chicago: Markham, 1971.

37. Kmenta, J. *Elements of Econometrics*. New York: Macmillan, 1971.

38. Lucas, Robert E. "Econometric Policy Evaluation: A Critique." In K. Brunner and A. Meltzer, eds. *Carnegie-Rochester Conference Series on Public Policy*. Vol. 1. New York: North Holland, 1976, pp. 19–46.

39. McNees, S. K. "An Evaluation of Economic Forecasts." *New England Economic Review*. Boston: Federal Reserve Bank of Boston, November/December 1975, pp. 3–39.

40. Marshak, J. "Statistical Inference in Economics, An Introduction." In T. C. Koopmans, ed. *Statistical Inference in Dynamic Economic Models*. New York: John Wiley, 1950.

41. Mincer, J., and V. Zarnowitz. "The Evaluation of Economic Forecasts." In J. Mincer, ed. *Economic Forecasts and Anticipations: Analyses of Forecasting Behavior and Performance*. New York: National Bureau of Economic Research, 1969, pp. 3–46.

42. Poirier, D. J. *The Econometrics of Structural Change*. New York: North Holland, 1976.

43. Schmidt, P. "The Asymptotic Distribution of Dynamic Multipliers." *Econometrica* 41 (1973): 161–164.

44. Shapiro, H. "Is Verification Possible? The Evaluation of Large Econometric Models." *Journal of Agricultural Economics* 55 (1973): 250–258.

45. Theil, H. *Economic Forecasts and Policy*. Amsterdam: North Holland, 1958.

46. Theil, H. *Principles of Econometrics*. New York: John Wiley, 1971.

47. Theil, H., and J. C. G. Boot. "The Final Form of Econometric Equation Systems." *Review of the International Statistical Institute* 30 (1962): 136–152.

48. Tinbergen, J. "Econometric Business Cycle Research." *Review of Economic Studies* 7 (1940): 73–90.

49. Tukey, J. *Exploratory Data Analysis*. Reading: Addison-Wesley, 1977.

50. Zaguskin, V. L. *Handbook of Numerical Methods for the Solution of Algebraic and Transcendental Equations*. New York: Pergamon Press, 1961.

51. Zarnowitz, V. *An Appraisal of Short-Term Economic Forecasts*. New York: National Bureau of Economic Research, 1967.

52. Zarnowitz, V. "Forecasting Economic Conditions: The Record and the Prospect." In V. Zarnowitz, ed. *The Business Cycle Today*. New York: National Bureau of Economic Research, 1972, pp. 183–239.

53. Zarnowitz, V. "How Well Do Economists Forecast Growth, Recession, and Inflation?" *Economic Outlook USA*. Ann Arbor: Survey Research Center of the University of Michigan, Spring 1978, pp. 22–25.

54. Zellner, A., and S. C. Peck. "Simulation Experiments with a Quarterly Macroeconometric Model of the U.S. Economy." In A. A. Powell and R. A. Williams, eds. *Econometric Studies of Macro and Monetary Relations*. New York: American Elsevier, 1973, pp. 149–168.

55. Zellner, A., and F. Palm. "Time Series Analysis and Simultaneous Equation Econometric Models." *Journal of Econometrics* 2 (1974): 17–54.

56. Zellner, A., and F. Palm. "Time Series and Structural Analysis of Monetary Models of the U.S. Economy." *Sankhya*, Series C, 37 (1975): 12–56.